ON THESE WALLS

Inscriptions and Quotations in the Buildings of the Library of Congress

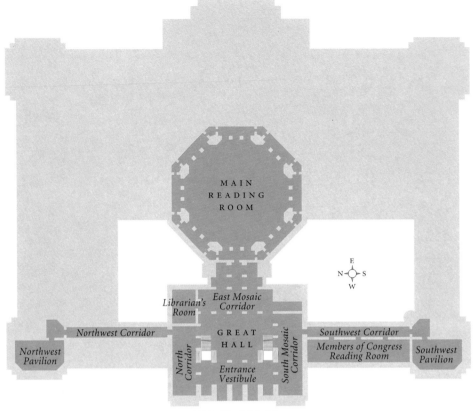

MAIN
READING
ROOM

*Librarian's
Room*

*East Mosaic
Corridor*

GREAT
HALL

*North
Corridor*

Northwest Corridor

*Northwest
Pavilion*

*South Mosaic
Corridor*

Southwest Corridor

*Members of Congress
Reading Room*

*Southwest
Pavilion*

*Entrance
Vestibule*

N–E·S–W

FIRST FLOOR

THOMAS JEFFERSON BUILDING FLOOR PLAN

SECOND FLOOR

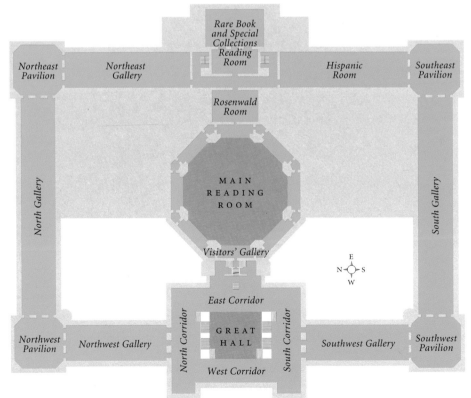

*Rare Book
and Special
Collections
Reading
Room*

*Northeast
Pavilion*

*Northeast
Gallery*

*Hispanic
Room*

*Southeast
Pavilion*

*Rosenwald
Room*

North Gallery

MAIN
READING
ROOM

South Gallery

Visitors' Gallery

N–E·S–W

East Corridor

*North
Corridor*

GREAT
HALL

*South
Corridor*

*Northwest
Pavilion*

Northwest Gallery

Southwest Gallery

*Southwest
Pavilion*

West Corridor

ON THESE WALLS

Inscriptions and Quotations in the Buildings of the Library of Congress

John Y. Cole

LIBRARY OF CONGRESS · WASHINGTON · 1995

THIS PUBLICATION WAS MADE POSSIBLE BY GENEROUS SUPPORT FROM THE JAMES MADISON COUNCIL, A NATIONAL, PRIVATE-SECTOR ADVISORY COUNCIL DEDICATED TO HELPING THE LIBRARY OF CONGRESS SHARE ITS UNIQUE RESOURCES WITH THE NATION AND THE WORLD

John Y. Cole is a librarian and historian who has been on the staff of the Library of Congress since 1966. He has been director of the Center for the Book since it was established in 1977.

LIBRARY OF CONGRESS CATALOGING-IN-PUBLICATION DATA

Cole, John Young, 1940–
    On these walls : inscriptions and quotations in the buildings of the Library of Congress / John Y. Cole.
        p.   cm.
    Includes bibliographical references and index.
    ISBN 0-8444-0485-X
    ——— ——— Copy 3 Z663 .05 1995
    1. Library of Congress — Buildings. 2. Library decoration — Washington (D.C.) 3. Architectural inscriptions — Washington (D.C.) 4. National libraries — Washington (D.C.) 5. Washington (D.C.) — Buildings, structures, etc. 6. Library architecture — Washington (D.C.) I. Library of Congress. II. Title.
Z733.U6C59 1995   92-24275
027.573 — dc20   CIP

Cover photograph and photos on pages 5, 8, and 14–15 by Carol M. Highsmith; photographs on pages 13 and 16, courtesy Office of the Architect of the Capitol.

Book design by Robert L. Wiser and Laurie Rosenthal, Meadows & Wiser, Washington, D.C.

For sale by the U.S. Government Printing Office
Superintendent of Documents, Mail Stop: SSOP, Washington, D.C. 20402-9328
ISBN 0-8444-0485-X

The U.S. Capitol, the home of the Library of Congress until 1897, is seen at sunrise through a window in the Jefferson Building's North Mosaic Corridor. A quotation from Confucius is being unfurled near the ceiling.

Cover: A quotation from Proverbs 4:7 in the Bible is paired with Robert Reid's painting Understanding *in the Jefferson Building's Great Hall (see pp. 62–63).*

Contents

❁ ❁

✿ ✿

VOSTRE

SIMON VOSTRE

THEY ARE NEVER ALONE
THAT ARE ACCOMPANIED
WITH NOBLE THOVGHTS.

Introduction

The three imposing buildings of the Library of Congress—the Thomas Jefferson Building, the John Adams Building, and the James Madison Memorial Building—are remarkable but very different public spaces and public works of art. Located just east of the U.S. Capitol Building, each in its own way is a powerful and impressive symbol of learning and democracy and of American culture and self-confidence. The inscriptions and quotations on the walls and ceilings of each building express the Library's ambitious mission of collecting and sharing the wisdom of all civilizations.

The Jefferson Building (1886–1897) is a reflection of a time that considered it possible to contain all knowledge within the walls of a single building. Designed and built in leaner times and primarily for functional purposes, the Adams (1930–1939) and Madison (1965–1980) Buildings nevertheless employ the words and symbols of history—and especially the words of the founding fathers.

"Summer," by Frank W. Benson, is one of the four seasons portrayed in the ceiling of the South Corridor on the second floor of the Jefferson Building's Great Hall. The printers' mark of the 16th century French printer Simon Vostre can be seen directly above the painting.

The architecture of the Library's buildings generally overpowers the inscriptions and quotations described in the pages that follow. Thus this book's purpose is to help visitors, especially in the Jefferson Building with its ebullient and often breathtaking interior, to locate, identify, and appreciate these names and phrases and their authors and creators.

Although the emphasis in the book is on words, not works of art, I cannot resist pointing out a few of the most memorable decorative features described in the pages that follow.

Outside of the Jefferson Building, the visitor should make a special point of spending a few minutes at the Neptune Fountain (p.21). In the Great Hall, the cherubs on the staircases and their various occupations are worth special attention, as are the classically-composed football and baseball players in the second floor Great Hall ceiling (p. 56); the symbolic and dominant figure of Minerva (p. 56), viewed as one ascends to view the Main Reading Room; and the remarkable "Evolution of Civilization" mural in the collar of the Main Reading Room's dome (p. 37). The owl, a symbol of wisdom, is seen throughout the decoration in the Jefferson Building and Adams Buildings; my favorites are the streamlined owls that stand guard on the stairs outside of the unused south entrance to the Adams Building (p. 79). A formidable and inspiring four-story high relief of cascading bronze books rises above the entrance to the Madison Building (p. 88).

The Thomas Jefferson Building opened on November 1, 1897. Soon thereafter, one admiring member of the public, Joseph E. Robinson, exclaimed to the Librarian of Congress: "not until I stand before the judgement seat of God do I ever expect to see this building transcended." My hope is that this guidebook will help others share at least a measure of Mr. Robinson's enthusiasm—for all of the Library's buildings.

NIL INVITA MINERVA QUAE MONUMENTUM
ÆRE PERENNIUS EXEGIT

A Brief History of the Library of Congress

❀ ❀

"Minerva," by Elihu Vedder, a marble mosaic on the landing of the stairs leading to the Visitors' Gallery above the Main Reading Room. Minerva is depicted as a guardian of civilization and promoter of the arts and sciences.

The oldest cultural institution in the nation's capital, the Library of Congress occupies a unique place in American civilization. Established as a legislative library in 1800, it grew into a national institution in the nineteenth century, a product of American cultural nationalism. Since World War II, it has become an international resource of unparalleled dimension and the world's largest library. In its three massive structures on Capitol Hill, the Thomas Jefferson, John Adams, and James Madison Memorial Buildings, the Library of Congress brings together the concerns of government, learning, and librarianship—an uncommon combination, but one that has greatly benefited American scholarship and culture.

The history of the Library of Congress is the story of the accumulation of diverse functions and collections. As a repository of information and knowledge, its collections in all formats now contain more than 103 million items—books (about 20 million), films, maps, photographs, music, manuscripts, and graphics—from all over the world. The scope of these collections is universal; materials have been acquired in more than four hundred and fifty languages. The Library is open to everyone over high school age, and more than two million tourists visit it annually.

The Library of Congress has been shaped primarily by the philosophy and ideas of its principal founder, Thomas Jefferson, who believed that a democratic legislature needed information and ideas on all subjects to do its work. It was established by Congress on April 24, 1800, with an appropriation of five thousand dollars, as the government prepared to move from Philadelphia to the new capital city of Washington. From the beginning, however, the institution was more than a legislative library, for an 1802 law made the appointment of the Librarian of Congress a presidential responsibility. It also permitted the president and vice president to borrow books, a privilege that eventually was extended to the judiciary, officials of government agencies, and, under certain conditions, members of the public. Originally located in the Capitol Building, the Library moved to its own building in 1897. At the same time, Congress gave the Librarian of Congress sole responsibility for making the Library's rules and regulations and invested in the Senate the authority to approve a president's nomination of a Librarian of Congress.

Thomas Jefferson took a keen and continuing interest in the Library. In 1814, when the British invaded Washington, they destroyed the Capitol, including the Library of Congress. By then retired to Monticello, Jefferson offered to sell his personal library of more than six thousand volumes to Congress. The purchase was approved in 1815, doubling the size of the Library. It also expanded the scope of the collections. Anticipating the argument that his collection might be too wide-ranging and comprehensive for use by a legislative body, Jefferson argued that there was "no subject to which a member of Congress may not have occasion to refer." The Jeffersonian concept of universality is the philosophy and rationale behind the comprehensive collecting policies of today's Library.

The individual responsible for transforming the Library of Congress into an institution of national significance was Ainsworth Rand Spofford, Librarian of Congress from 1864 to 1897. Spofford applied Jefferson's philosophy on a grand scale. He linked the Library's legislative and national functions, building a comprehensive collection for both the legislature and the nation. In obtaining greatly increased support from Congress, Spofford employed a combination of logic, flattery, and nationalistic rhetoric. In 1867 his acquisitions made the Library of Congress the largest library in the United States. Spofford's other major achievements were the centralization in 1870 of all U.S. copyright activities at the Library—which ensured the continuing growth of the collections by stipulating that two copies of every book, pamphlet, map, print, and piece of music registered for copyright be deposited in the Library—and construction of a separate building, a twenty-six year struggle not completed until 1897.

Spofford's concept of the Library of Congress as both legislative library for the American Congress and national library for the American people has been wholeheartedly accepted by his successors. Herbert Putnam, Librarian of Congress from 1899 to 1939, extended this philosophy still fur-

Francis Bacon is one of the great authors whose name appears in the vaulted cove of the ceiling of the Great Hall in the Jefferson Building. The date "1896" and name of the painter, Frederic C. Martin, can be seen in the upper left corner.

ther. To Putnam, a national library was more than a comprehensive collection housed in Washington. It was "a collection universal in scope which has a duty to the country as a whole." He defined that duty as service to scholarship, both directly and through other libraries.

The first experienced librarian to fill the position, Putnam felt that a national library should actively serve other libraries, and he immediately began such a service. Through the sale and distribution of printed catalog cards, union catalogs, interlibrary loan, and other innovations, he "nationalized" the Library's collections and established the patterns of service that exist today. During his tenure, the Library helped systemize American scholarship and librarianship through the widespread sharing of its bibliographic apparatus, thus encouraging a national view of scholarship and research collections and establishing pioneering partnerships between the federal government and the private sector.

Balancing its legislative, national, and, after World War II, international roles, the Library of Congress has grown steadily. Historically, its major problem has been lack of space, not lack of support. Librarian of Congress Archibald MacLeish (1939–1944) stressed the Library's roles as a symbol of democracy and a cultural institution. Luther H. Evans (1945–1953) pushed forward the Library's bibliographic and international activities. L. Quincy Mumford (1954–1974) greatly expanded all the Library's roles, but particularly its bibliographic activities and foreign acquisitions.

A new public role for the Library began to emerge under the leadership of historian Daniel J. Boorstin, Librarian of Congress, 1975–1987. Emphasizing the Library's role as a national cultural resource, he greatly increased the institution's visibility. Boorstin's successor in 1987, historian James H. Billington, has vigorously pursued a similar course. He also has established private sector support groups and an educational role for the Library, using new technologies to share the Library's collections with the nation. As it approaches its bicentennial in the year 2000, the Library of Congress is still guided by Thomas Jefferson's belief that information and knowledge about all subjects are essential in a democracy—for legislators and citizens alike.

FORTITVDE

JVSTICE

The Thomas Jefferson Building

✤ ✤

Pompeiian panels depicting FORTITUDE *and* JUSTICE *flank the window at the east end of the Great Hall's second-floor North Corridor. The artist is George Maynard.*

Pages 14–15: The grandiose entrance stairs and facade of the west side of the Jefferson Building reflect the nationalistic ambitions of the Library's planners, architects, and builders.

The Library of Congress was established in 1800 when the American government moved from Philadelphia to the new capital of Washington on the Potomac River. For 97 years the Library was housed in various locations within the Capitol Building. The first separate Library of Congress Building, known today as the Thomas Jefferson Building, was suggested by Librarian of Congress Ainsworth Rand Spofford in 1871, authorized in 1886, and finally completed in 1897.

When its doors were opened to the public on November 1, 1897, the new Library of Congress building was an unparalleled national achievement; its 23-carat gold-plated dome capped the "largest, costliest, and safest" library building in the world. Its elaborately decorated facade and interior, for which more than forty American painters and sculptors produced commissioned works of art, were designed to show how the United States could surpass European libraries in grandeur and devotion to classical culture and to inspire optimism about America's future. A contemporary guidebook boasted: "America is justly proud of this gorgeous and palatial monument to its National sympathy and appreciation of Literature, Science, and Art. It has been designed and executed solely by American art and American labor and is a fitting tribute for the great thoughts of generations past, present, and to be." This new national Temple of the Arts immediately met with overwhelming approval from the American public.

Known as the Library of Congress (or Main) Building until June 13, 1980, when it was named for Thomas Jefferson, the Library's principal founder, the structure was built specifically to serve as the American national library, and its architecture and decoration express and enhance that grand purpose. The elaborate entrance pavilion and Great Hall gradually lead to the central reading room where, properly prepared, the user can take full advantage of the Library's vast resources of knowledge and information. A national library for the United States was the dream and goal of Librarian Spofford; the new building was a crucial step in his achievement. It was a functional, state-of-the-art structure as well as a monument to American cultural nationalism, for it used and celebrated the latest technology to demonstrate the new role of the library as an efficient workshop.

The early years of planning and construction were filled with controversy and delay. After two design competitions and a decade of debate about design and location, in 1886 Congress finally chose a plan in the Italian Renaissance style submitted by Washington architects John L. Smithmeyer and Paul J. Pelz. Structurally the architects followed the basic idea proposed by Librarian Spofford: a circular, domed reading room at the Library's center, surrounded by ample space for the Library's various departments. In the final Smithmeyer & Pelz plan, the reading room was enclosed by rectangular exterior walls, which divided the open space into four courtyards. The corner pavilions were devoted to the departments and to exhibit space.

Disputes continued after the building was authorized in 1886. Responsibility for clearing the site was debated (several buildings had to be razed) and Capitol landscape architect Frederick Law Olmsted protested the building's location because it shut out "the whole view of the Capitol building from Pennsylvania Avenue—the main approach from Capitol hill." Another controversy, this one about the selection of the proper cement for the foundation, proved to be architect Smithmeyer's undoing, and he was dismissed in 1888. The building's construction was placed under the direction of Brig. Gen. Thomas Lincoln Casey, Chief of the U.S. Army Corps of Engineers. Casey and his Superintendent of Construction, civil engineer Bernard R. Green, had successfully completed the construction of the Washington Monument and the State, War, and Navy (now Old Executive Office) Building and were

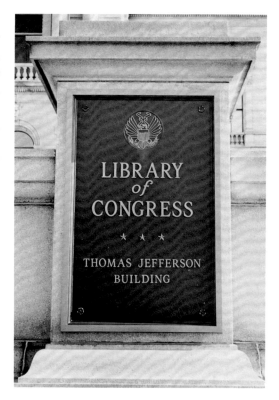

Plaque on First Street S.E. in front of the Jefferson Building. The Library of Congress seal is above the inscription. The Jefferson Building acquired its name in 1980.

trusted by Congress. The cornerstone was laid on Aug. 28, 1890. Paul J. Pelz, who replaced Smithmeyer as architect in 1888, was himself dismissed in 1892 and replaced by architect Edward Pearce Casey, General Casey's son, who supervised most of the interior decoration.

The building's elaborate decoration, which combines sculpture, mural painting, and architecture on a scale unsurpassed in any American public building, was possible only because General Casey and Bernard Green lived up to their reputations as efficient construction engineers, completing the building for a sum substantially less than that appropriated by Congress. When it became apparent in 1892 that funds for "artistic enrichment" would be available out of the original appropriation, Casey and Green seized the opportunity and turned an already remarkable building into a cultural monument.

The two engineers were infused with a nationalism that complemented Spofford's national library aspirations. The 1893 World's Columbian Exposition in Chicago provided General Casey, his architect son Edward, and Bernard Green with an example of a cooperative artistic endeavor that combined architecture, sculpture, and painting, and there are many similarities and parallels between the Chicago Exposition and the Library building. Both are artistic ventures on a massive scale and, for the most part, in the same Beaux-Arts design tradition. Many of the artists who contributed works to the Library building either helped design the imperial facades of the Chicago Exposition or exhibited their works within its pavilions; moreover, many of them repeated the idealistic themes and togaed likenesses they produced in Chicago.

General Casey and Bernard Green were anxious to give American artists an opportunity to display their talents, and ultimately they commissioned no less than forty-two American sculptors and painters "to fully and consistently carry out the monumental design and purpose of the building." Casey and Green exercised final approval over the words and images seen throughout the building, even though the names, inscriptions, and quotations were chosen by many different people.

The works of art were expected to address various areas of human achievement without getting into controversial areas such as politics and religion. The sculptors were assigned general themes, but the muralists, with guidance from the two engineers and Edward Pearce Casey, chose their own themes and, it appears, most of the inscriptions and quotations within their assigned areas. Librarian Spofford chose the authors (his favorites) who are portrayed in the nine busts in the portico above the front entrance (see p. 22), and the quotations in the Pavilion of Seals (the Northeast Pavilion). He also chose the figures portrayed in the sixteen portrait statues on the balustrade of the Main Reading Room (see p. 35) and, in all likelihood, the quotations in the four corridors on the second floor of the Great Hall. Charles W. Eliot, president of Harvard University, chose the inscriptions above the eight symbolic statues in the Main Reading Room (see p. 33), and provided the Caseys and Bernard Green with advice about other inscriptions and decorative features.

In a report to Congress in 1896, Superintendent Green stated that the total cost of the mural and decorative painting, the sculpture, and the three massive bronze doors at the main entrance was $364,000. Even with the additional costs of gilding the building's dome, including the Torch of Learning at its apex, and the construction of the Neptune Fountain in front of the building on First Street, the building was completed for $200,000 less than the total congressional authorization of approximately $6,500,000.

Weather and the chemical effects of the 19th century method of tinning the copper beneath the gold leaf dome combined to produce perforations in the copper in the 20th century, and the leaking gilded copper was replaced in October 1931. It was thought that gold leaf would conflict with the appearance of the building's aging granite exterior, and the new copper was left to acquire its current patina. In August 1993, however, the flame of the Torch of Learning at the apex of the dome was regilded, this time with 23½ carat gold leaf.

Since 1897, three of the four interior courtyards of the Jefferson Building have been filled. The east courtyards have become bookstacks; the southeast bookstack was completed in 1910, the northeast in 1927. The northwest courtyard is occupied by two special structures: the Coolidge Auditorium, built in 1925 for chamber music recitals and a gift of Elizabeth Sprague Coolidge, and the Whittall Pavilion, given to the Library in 1938 by Gertrude Clarke Whittall to house five Stradivarius instruments she donated to the Library. A plaque commemorating Mrs. Coolidge and her gift is outside the entrance to the Coolidge Auditorium, on the ground floor. The names of four great composers—Mozart, Beethoven, Schubert, Brahms—are inscribed on the outside wall of the Whittall Pavilion, above the windows and the stairs leading down to the interior courtyard.

The east side of the Jefferson Building was extended between 1929 and 1933, providing space for a Rare Book Room, a Union Catalog Room, and additional study rooms.

In 1924 a marble and bronze exhibit case known as the Shrine, designed by architect Francis Bacon, was installed on the west side of the second floor gallery in the Great Hall. There the Declaration of Independence and the Constitution of the United States were displayed until 1952 when the documents were transferred to the National Archives. As part of the restoration that began in 1986, the empty Shrine was removed from the Great Hall and placed into storage.

The Main Reading Room was closed for renovation and the installation of air conditioning on May 4, 1964, reopening on August 16, 1965. In 1984, Congress appropriated $81.5 million for the renovation and restoration of the

Jefferson and Adams Buildings, which included the cleaning and conservation of murals in the Jefferson Building. Work started in 1986 and was completed in 1995.

The Jefferson Building is a heroic setting for a national institution. Today it is recognized as a unique blending of art and architecture, a structure that celebrates learning, nationalism, and American turn-of-the-century confidence and optimism. The Jefferson Building also reflects its own time and prejudices. It emphasizes the achievements of western civilization, and most of the names and images on its walls evoke a society dominated by western thought. Thus, for many different reasons, the elaborate embellishment of the Jefferson Building is worth careful attention. The building is celebratory, inspirational, and educational. Few structures represent human aspiration in such dramatic fashion.

THE WEST FRONT EXTERIOR

The Neptune Fountain

This lavishly ornamental fountain, created by sculptor Roland Hinton Perry, represents a scene in the court of Neptune, the Roman god of the sea. The muscular and majestic Neptune, with his long flowing beard, is seated on a bank of rocks. The figure is of colossal size; if standing, it would be about twelve feet in height. On each side of Neptune lolls a figure of Triton, one of the minor sea gods, blowing a conch shell to summon the water deities to Neptune's throne. Sea nymphs, sea horses, sea monsters, gigantic frogs, and huge turtles are part of this extraordinary and splendid grotto of the sea. Perry's name and the date he completed the work are inscribed to the right of Neptune, at the fountain's water level.

The Ethnological Heads

One of the Jefferson Building's most striking exterior features are the thirty-three ethnological heads that surround it, serving as keystone ornaments of the first story windows. Otis T. Mason, curator of the Department of Ethnology in the National Museum of Natural History, Smithsonian Institution, was the special advisor for this project. In Herbert Small's 1897 *Handbook of the New Library of Congress,* this undertaking is described as "the first instance of a comprehensive attempt to make ethnological science contribute to the architectural decoration of an important public building." The heads themselves, created by William Boyd and Henry Jackson Ellicott, were based on information provided by Professor Mason. The list of the races represented, as described by Small, and the location of the keystones follow.

Starting at the north end of the front entrance pavilion, the first head is that of a Russian Slav, located beneath the portico bust of Demosthenes. Continuing across the west front, the heads are: Blonde European; Brunette European; Modern Greek; Persian (Iranian);

On the south side: Circassian; Hindu; Hungarian (Magyar); Semite, or Jew; Arab (Bedouin); Turk

On the east side: Modern Egyptian (Hamite); Abyssinian; Malay; Polynesian; Australian; Negrito (Indian Archipeligo); Sudan Negro; Akka (Dwarf African Negro); Fuegian; Botocudo (South America); Pueblo Indian (Zunis of New Mexico);

On the north side: Esquimaux; Plains Indians (Sioux, Cheyenne, Comanche); Samoyede (Finn); Korean; Japanese; Ainu (northern Japan);

On the west front: Burman; Tibetan; Chinese

The Portico Busts

In the portico of the Jefferson Building's front entrance pavilion—at second story window level—nine great men are commemorated by busts. Benjamin Franklin was placed in the center of this grouping, because he was considered by the sculptor Frederick Wellington Ruckstuhl to be "one of the greatest men of this country, and as a writer and philosopher the patriarch." Each last name is inscribed at the base of the bust. Franklin and the eight others who were so enshrined are listed below, along with the name of the sculptors of each bust.

Ainsworth Rand Spofford, Librarian of Congress 1864–1897, chose his favorite authors to be portrayed by busts on the Jefferson Building's portico, facing the Capitol. Pictured opposite is Dante, by sculptor Herbert Adams.

North end of portico:
DEMOSTHENES, by Herbert Adams

Across the front (left to right)
EMERSON, by Jonathan Scott Hartley
IRVING, by Jonathan Scott Hartley
GOETHE, by Frederick Wellington Ruckstull
FRANKLIN, by Frederick Wellington Ruckstull
MACAULAY, by Frederick Wellington Ruckstull
HAWTHORNE, by Jonathan Scott Hartley
SCOTT, by Herbert Adams

South end of portico:
DANTE, by Herbert Adams

The Jefferson Building opened in 1897, eleven years after its construction was authorized, and 26 years after Librarian Spofford called for a separate Library building.

The Construction Dates

Dates marking the beginning and end of the construction of the Jefferson Building are carved in the granite exterior at the ground level on the north end of the portico (1889) and the south end (1897). The cornerstone, containing documents about the history of the building, was laid without ceremony on August 28, 1890, on the ground level in the northeast corner. The inscription, "AUGUST 28, 1890," was put on the stone on January 16, 1952.

The Entrance Porch

The Main Entrance to the Jefferson Building is at the top of the imposing front stairway and through an entrance porch of three arches into the Great Hall at the first floor level. The six life-size spandrel figures leaning gracefully against the curve of each of the arches were sculpted by Bela Lyon Pratt. They represent Literature (the left-hand arch), Science (the center arch) and Art (the right-hand arch). Of the two figures representing Literature, the left one holds a writing tablet and the right one holds a book while gazing into the distance. Of the two figures representing Science, the first holds the torch of Knowledge, and the second looks upward, thus repeating, in a general way, the distinction between the practical and the abstract seen in the left-hand door. In the third group, the figure to the left represents Sculpture (he's working on a bust of Dante), and the one to the right represents Painting.

24

The Bronze Doors

The three arches of the Entrance Porch end at three massive bronze doors covered with a design of rich sculptural ornament. Each is a double door, 14 feet high to the top of the arch, and weighs about three and one-half tons. The subjects and the sculptors are, from left to right: *Tradition,* modeled by Olin Levi Warner; *The Art of Printing,* by Frederick MacMonnies; and *Writing,* by Olin Levi Warner, which though unfinished at his death in August 1896, was completed by Herbert Adams. Taken together as a sequential series, Tradition, Writing, and Printing, illustrate the successive and, according to Small's *Handbook,* the "gradually more perfect" ways that humans have preserved religion, history, literature, and science.

Tradition (left-hand door)

Tradition illustrates how knowledge was originally handed down from generation to generation. In the lunette above the door, an American Indian, a Norseman, a prehistoric man, and a shepherd listen intently to the words of the central figure. Each of these lunette figures represents peoples who kept their history alive via oral tradition. The face of the Indian was taken from a sketch of Chief Joseph of the Nez Percé tribe that sculptor Warner made in 1889. (The compiler of a contemporary guidebook, Charles B. Reynolds, asserts that on the day in April 1897 when he was making notes on the door, "Chief Joseph himself was here at the Library, looking upon this portrait of himself.") The names of the artist and the door's foundry can be seen at the bottom of the lunette.

The figures on the large door panels below the lunette represent Imagination (on the left) and Memory (on the right). Sculptor Warner's signature and the date of the work can be seen near the left foot of Imagination and the right foot of Memory. The word "Tradition," engraved on a medallion on the reverse side of the lunette, can be seen from inside the entrance.

The Art of Printing (center door)

Frederick MacMonnies entitled the lunette above the door "Minerva Diffusing the Products of Typographical Art." Minerva, the Roman goddess of learning and wisdom, is seated in the center. The Latin title of the subject, *Ars Typographica,* and various symbolic ornaments can be seen in the background. The figures on the door panels below represent the Humanities (on the left) and Intellect (on the right). The artist has signed his work on the doors near the feet of Intellect. The phrase "Homage to Gutenberg," engraved on the reverse side of the lunette, can be seen from inside the entrance.

Writing (right-hand door)

In the lunette above the doors, the four figures surrounding the central figure represent people who have influenced the world through their written liter-

The Gutenberg Bible

ERECTED UNDER THE ACTS OF CONGRESS OF
APRIL 15·1886 OCTOBER 2·1888 AND MARCH 2·1889 BY
BRIG·GEN·THOS· LINCOLN CASEY
CHIEF OF ENGINEERS U·S·A·

BERNARD R·GREEN SUPT·AND ENGINEER
JOHN L·SMITHMEYER ARCHITECT
PAUL J·PELZ ARCHITECT
EDWARD PEARCE CASEY ARCHITECT

LIBRARY OF CONGRESS

ature: an Egyptian and a Jew on the right, and a Christian and a Greek on the left. The figures on the door panels below represent Truth (on the left) and Research (on the right). As the inscription on the right side of the doors indicates, this work was begun by Olin Levi Warner, who died in 1896, and completed by Herbert Adams.

The Entrance Vestibule

Even though many visitors first view the Great Hall after climbing the stairs from the Library's ground floor entrance, the Great Hall was designed so that the most spectacular view awaits those who enter through the bronze doors at the first floor west entrance. From here one steps into the sumptuously decorated main vestibule, with its gleaming white marble arches, stucco decoration, and heavily-paneled and gold-ornamented ceiling. As your eye travels up the short piers to the gilt ceiling you see the paired figures of Minerva, created by Herbert Adams as the "Minerva of War" and the "Minerva of Peace" and placed atop each marble pillar at the base of the double staircases. "Minerva of War" grasps a short sword in one hand and holds aloft the torch of learning in the other; "Minerva of Peace" holds a globe, which symbolizes the universal scope of knowledge, and a scroll.

The Minerva mosaic, the Gutenberg Bible exhibit, and the arch commemorating the construction of the Jefferson Building are captured in this photograph of the east side of the Great Hall taken in the 1950s.

A plaque on the central pillar commemorates Daniel Wolsey Voorhees (1827–1897), a Senator from Indiana. Voorhees strongly supported Librarian Spofford's campaign to construct a separate Library building. The inscription reads:

AS A MEMBER FOR EIGHTEEN YEARS OF THE JOINT COMMITTEE ON THE LIBRARY, AS CHAIRMAN FOR SEVENTEEN YEARS OF THE JOINT SELECT COMMITTEE ON ADDITIONAL ACCOMMODATIONS FOR THE LIBRARY, AND IN MANY ELOQUENT PLEAS ON THE FLOOR OF THE SENATE, HE TOOK A LEADING PART IN OBTAINING THIS LIBRARY BUILDING FOR THE AMERICAN PEOPLE

The Floors

The flooring in the entrance vestibule is made of white Italian marble, with bands and geometric patterns of brown Tennessee marble. Modeling and incised brass inlays have been added to the marble floor within the Great Hall. In the center of the floor is the sun, on which are noted the four cardinal points of the compass. These compass points correspond to directions within the Library—e.g., the Main Reading Room is to the east. Should you become confused about the location of any of the Jefferson

Building's features mentioned in this guidebook, please refer to this compass to get your bearings.

The inlays represent the twelve signs of the zodiac, beginning with Leo in the northwest corner. Proceeding clockwise, the others are: Cancer, Gemini, Taurus, Aries, Pisces, Aquarius, Capricorn, Sagittarius, Scorpio, Libra, and Virgo.

The Commemorative Arch

The arcade at the center of the east side of the Great Hall takes the form of a triumphant arch commemorating the construction of the building. The words LIBRARY OF CONGRESS are inscribed in tall gilt letters above the arch. A marble tablet inscribed with the names of the building's construction engineers and architects is part of the parapet immediately above. The tablet, flanked by two majestic eagles, reads:

ERECTED UNDER THE ACTS OF CONGRESS OF APRIL 15 1886, OCTOBER 2 1888 AND MARCH 2 1889 BY BRIG. GEN. THOS. LINCOLN CASEY CHIEF OF ENGINEERS U.S.A. BERNARD R. GREEN SUPT. AND ENGINEER JOHN L. SMITHMEYER ARCHITECT PAUL J. PELZ ARCHITECT EDWARD PEARCE CASEY ARCHITECT

The spandrels of the arch beneath the inscriptions contain two signed sculptured figures by Olin Levi Warner titled *The Students*. The figure on the left is a youth seeking to acquire knowledge from books. On the right, an old sage is engaged in thought and reflection.

The elaborate ornamentation of the Great Hall, which has been called "the richest interior in America," is highlighted in this photograph taken in the 1960s.

The Staircases

The two great staircases flanking the Great Hall are embellished by elaborate and varied sculptural work by Philip Martiny. At the base of each is a bronze female figure wearing classic drapery and holding a torch of knowledge. They are signed "P H Martiny, sculptor NY"; the foundry's name is also inscribed at the base. Each stair railing is decorated with a fanciful series of cherubs carved by Martiny in white marble. In a niche on the north side is a plaster bust of Thomas Jefferson and on the south is a bronze bust of George Washington; both are copied from works by the sculptor Jean-Antoine Houdon. The balustrade on each side of the top landing contains Martiny's figures of cherubs modeled to represent the fine arts. At the north landing, they are *Painting, Architecture,* and *Sculpture;* at the south landing, *Comedy, Poetry,* and *Tragedy.*

The cherubs in the ascending railing of each staircase—according to Small's *Handbook*—represent "the various occupations, habits, and pursuits of modern life." The series begins at the bottom with the figure of a stork. Then, on the north side of the hall, are figures of a *Gardener,* with a spade and

a rake; an *Entomologist,* capturing butterflies; a *Student* poring over a text; a *Printer,* with typefaces, a type case, and a press. Halfway up the railing, on the same level, are cherubs representing *Asia* and *Europe.* Next comes a *Musician;* a *Physician,* mortar and pestle in hand; and an *Electrician* holding a telephone receiver at his ear and, Small writes, "with a star of electric rays shining on his brow." At the top of the railing is an *Astronomer* with a telescope.

In the staircase railing on the south side of the Great Hall, beginning at the bottom, the figures are a *Mechanic* with a cogwheel and pincers; a *Hunter,* with a gun, hoisting a rabbit he has just shot; a *Vintner* dressed like Bacchus, the Roman god of wine, holding a goblet; a *Farmer* with a sickle and a sheaf of wheat. Halfway up the railing are cherubs representing *Africa* and *America.* Next comes a *Fisherman;* a *Soldier,* a *Chemist,* with a blowpipe; and, last but not least, a *Cook.*

The Ceiling

The names of ten great authors can be seen on tablets above the Great Hall's semicircular latticed windows in the vaulted cove of the ceiling. Beginning on the east and proceeding clockwise, the names are DANTE, HOMER, MILTON, BACON, ARISTOTLE, GOETHE, SHAKESPEARE, MOLIERE, MOSES, and HERODOTUS. The names of eight more authors are inscribed in gilt letters on tablets beneath the second-story cartouches on the east and west sides of the hall. Beginning on the east and reading left to right, the authors are CERVANTES, HUGO, SCOTT, COOPER, LONGFELLOW, TENNYSON, GIBBON, and BANCROFT.

THE EAST MOSAIC CORRIDOR AND ENTRANCE TO THE MAIN READING ROOM

Adorning the East Corridor are six lunettes by John White Alexander that depict *The Evolution of the Book.* The subjects are, at the south end, the *Cairn, Oral Tradition,* and *Egyptian Hieroglyphics;* and, at the north end, *Picture Writing,* the *Manuscript Book,* and the *Printing Press.*

In the vault mosaics, at the ends and along the sides, are ten trophies, each with symbols representing one of the arts or sciences. Below each are the surnames of two native-born Americans associated with that art or science. Beginning on the east wall and reading left to right, they are: MATHEMATICS (Peirce and Bowditch), ASTRONOMY (Bond and Rittenhouse), ENGINEERING (Francis and Stevens), NATURAL PHILOSOPHY (Silliman and Cooke), ARCHITECTURE (Latrobe and Walter), MUSIC (Mason and Gottschalk), PAINTING (Stuart and Allston), SCULPTURE (Powers and Crawford), POETRY (Emerson and Holmes), and NATURAL SCIENCE (Say and Dana).

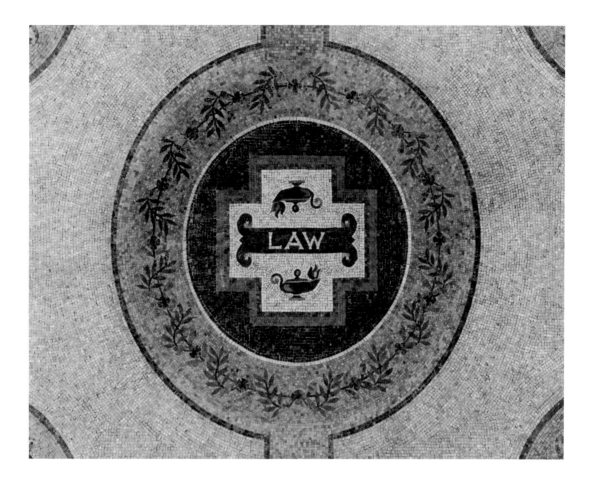

"Law" is one of 13 fields of knowledge celebrated in the East Mosaic Corridor near the first floor entrance to the Main Reading Room.

Names of native-born Americans distinguished in Medicine, Law, and Theology are inscribed in the ceiling vault. Beginning at the north end, they are: THEOLOGY (Brooks, Edwards, Mather, Channing, Beecher); LAW (Shaw, Taney, Marshall, Story, Gibson, Pinckney, Kent, Hamilton, Webster, Curtis); and MEDICINE (Cross, Wood, McDowell, Rush, Warren).

At either end of the East Corridor a stairway leads to the ground floor. In the domed lobbies at the head of each stairway are these quotations:

North lobby:

KNOWLEDGE IS POWER

Sir Francis Bacon, De Hoeresibus

South lobby:

E PLURIBUS UNUM [One From Many]

Horace, Epistle *ii, 212.*

Five small but stunning paintings by Elihu Vedder grace the lunettes at the entrance to the Main Reading Room. (Each is copyrighted by the artist along the lower edge.) This strategically-placed series and its subject *Government* are of special importance. As Herbert Small notes in his *Handbook,* "In every sort of library the fundamental thing is the advancement of learning—illustrated in the Reading Room dome, as the visitor will see later—but in a library supported by the nation the idea of government certainly comes next in importance."

In the painting above the central door to the Reading Room, titled *Government* and representing the ideal state, one can see the figure of Good Government holding a plaque on which is inscribed a quote from Abraham Lincoln's Gettysburg Address, "A government of the people, by the people, and for the people." Two paintings explaining the practical working of government flank each side of this central image. To the left, *Corrupt Legislation* leads to *Anarchy* (the scroll of learning is burning in Anarchy's right hand, and she is trampling on a scroll, a lyre, a Bible, and a book); to the right, *Good Administration* (the youth on the right, educated by the books he is carrying, is casting his ballot into the urn) leads to *Peace and Prosperity.*

"Government" by Elihu Vedder, in the central lunette over the door leading to the Main Reading Room, represents the abstract conception of a republic as the ideal state.

Visitors should take the elevators to the third floor to view the Main Reading Room from the Visitors' Gallery, or walk up the two flights of marble stairs.

The Eight Symbolic Statues and Their Inscriptions

From the Visitors' Gallery, eight large statues can be seen above the giant marble columns that surround the reading room. They represent eight categories of knowledge, each considered symbolic of civilized life and thought. Their titles are inscribed in gilt letters on a tablet in the frieze below them. Beginning with the figures on the east side of the room—from the perspective of the Visitor's Gallery—the symbolic statues are: *Philosophy*, by Bela Lyon Pratt; *Art*, by François M. L. Tonetti-Dozzi (after sketches by Augustus St. Gaudens); *History*, by Daniel Chester French; *Commerce*, by John Flanagan; *Religion*, by Theodore Baur; *Science*, by John Donoghue; *Law*, by Paul Wayland Bartlett; and *Poetry*, by John Quincy Adams Ward.

Above each statue is a large tablet bearing an inscription in gilt letters. Each of the eight inscriptions, appropriate to the subject of the statue below it, was chosen by Harvard University President Charles W. Eliot.

Above the figure of *Philosophy:*
THE INQUIRY, KNOWLEDGE, AND BELIEF OF TRUTH
IS THE SOVEREIGN GOOD OF HUMAN NATURE.
Bacon, Essays, *"Of Truth"*

Above the figure of *Art:*
AS ONE LAMP LIGHTS ANOTHER, NOR GROWS LESS,
SO NOBLENESS ENKINDLETH NOBLENESS.
Lowell, Yussouf

Above the figure of *History:*
ONE GOD, ONE LAW, ONE ELEMENT, AND ONE FAR-OFF DIVINE EVENT,
TO WHICH THE WHOLE CREATION MOVES
Tennyson, In Memoriam

Above the figure of *Commerce:*
WE TASTE THE SPICES OF ARABIA YET NEVER FEEL
THE SCORCHING SUN WHICH BRINGS THEM FORTH.
Anon. [Dudley North, East India Trade*]*

Above the figure of *Religion:*

WHAT DOTH THE LORD REQUIRE OF THEE, BUT TO DO JUSTLY,
AND TO LOVE MERCY, AND TO WALK HUMBLY WITH THY GOD?

Holy Bible, Micah 6:8

Above the figure of *Science:*

THE HEAVENS DECLARE THE GLORY OF GOD;
AND THE FIRMAMENT SHEWETH HIS HANDIWORK.

Holy Bible, Psalms 19:1

Above the figure of *Law:*

OF LAW THERE CAN BE NO LESS ACKNOWLEDGED
THAN THAT HER VOICE IS THE HARMONY OF THE WORLD.

Richard Hooker

Above the figure of *Poetry:*

HITHER, AS TO THEIR FOUNTAIN, OTHER STARS REPAIRING,
IN THEIR GOLDEN URNS DRAW LIGHT.

Milton, Paradise Lost, *vii, 364*

The Athenian states-man, lawgiver, and reformer Solon is one of two bronze statues that portrays "law" in the Main Reading Room. The scroll in his hand bears the Greek words OI NOMOI *("the law"). The sculptor is Frederick Wellington Ruckstull.*

The Sixteen Bronze Statues

Sixteen bronze statues set along the balustrade of the galleries represent men renowned for their accomplishments in the categories of knowledge and activity described above. The subjects were chosen by Ainsworth Rand Spofford, Librarian of Congress 1864–1897. The statues are paired, each pair flanking one of the eight giant marble columns. The names of individual figures are inscribed on the wall directly behind the statue. The list of those selected as representatives of human thought and civilization follows, along with the name of the sculptor of each statue.

Philosophy

PLATO and BACON. Both by John Joseph Boyle

Art

MICHAELANGELO, by Paul Wayland Bartlett
BEETHOVEN, by Theodore Baur

History

HERODOTUS, by Daniel Chester French
GIBBON, by Charles H. Niehaus

Commerce

COLUMBUS, by Paul Wayland Bartlett
FULTON, by Edward Clark Potter

Religion

ST. PAUL, by John Donoghue
MOSES, by Charles H. Niehaus

Science

NEWTON, by Cyrus Edwin Dallin
HENRY, by Herbert Adams

Law

SOLON, by Frederick Wellington Ruckstull
KENT, by George Edwin Bissell

Poetry

SHAKESPEARE, by Frederick MacMonnies
HOMER, by Louis Saint-Gaudens

The State Seals

The seals of the states of the union at the time the Jefferson Building was constructed are contained in the massive semicircular stained glass windows that surround the Main Reading Room. At the top, in the middle of each of the eight windows, is the Great Seal of the United States. To the right and left, following the curve of each window, are the seals of the states and territories, three on a side, six in each window. Thus, forty-eight seals are included.

The name of the state or territory is inscribed above each seal, along with the date of the year in which it was admitted to the Union or organized under a territorial form of government. The seals are displayed in the order of their dates. The series begins in the west window (above and behind the Visitors' Gallery).

Above the bronze statues of Moses and Newton are the seals: Delaware, 1787; Pennsylvania, 1787; New Jersey, 1787; Georgia, 1788; Connecticut, 1788; Massachusetts, 1788.

Proceeding clockwise, in the northwest window, above the bronze statues of Henry and Solon, are: Maryland, 1788; South Carolina, 1788; New Hampshire, 1788; Virginia, 1788; New York, 1788; North Carolina, 1789.

In the north window, above the bronze statues of Kent and Shakespeare, are: Rhode Island, 1790; Vermont, 1791; Kentucky, 1792; Tennessee, 1796; Ohio, 1802; Louisiana, 1812.

In the northeast window, above the bronze statues of Homer and Plato, are: Indiana, 1816; Mississippi, 1817; Illinois, 1818; Alabama, 1819; Maine, 1820; Missouri 1821.

In the east window, above the bronze statues of Bacon and Michelangelo, are the seals: Arkansas, 1836; Michigan, 1837; Florida, 1845; Texas, 1845; Iowa, 1846; Wisconsin, 1848.

In the southeast window, above the statues of Beethoven and Herodotus, are: California, 1850; Minnesota, 1858; Oregon, 1859; Kansas, 1861; West Virginia, 1863; Nevada, 1864.

In the south window, above the bronze statues of Gibbon and Columbus, are: Nebraska, 1867; Colorado, 1876; North Dakota, 1889; South Dakota, 1889; Montana, 1889; Washington, 1889.

In the southwest window, above the bronze statues of Fulton and St. Paul, are: Idaho, 1890; Wyoming, 1890; Utah, 1895; New Mexico, 1850 (territory); Arizona, 1863 (territory); Oklahoma, 1890 (territory).

The Paintings in the Dome

Edwin Howland Blashfield's murals, which adorn the dome of the Main Reading Room, occupy the central and the highest point of the building and form the culmination of the entire interior decorative scheme. The round mural set inside the lantern of the dome depicts *Human Understanding*, looking upward beyond the finite intellectual achievements represented by the twelve figures in the collar of the dome.

These twelve seated figures represent the twelve countries, or epochs, which Blashfield felt contributed most to American civilization. To the immediate right of each figure is a tablet on which is inscribed the name of the country typified and, below this, the name of the outstanding contribution of that country to human progress.

The figures follow each other in chronological order, beginning in the east, the cradle of civilization. The figures and their respective inscriptions are:

EGYPT: WRITTEN RECORDS. The personal seal of Mena, the first Egyptian King, is inscribed in hieroglypics in the tablet.

JUDEA: RELIGION. On the face of the pillar is inscribed, in Hebrew characters, the injunction: Thou shalt love they neighbor as thyself. (Holy Bible, Leviticus 19:18)

GREECE: PHILOSOPHY

ROME: ADMINISTRATION

ISLAM: PHYSICS

THE MIDDLE AGES: MODERN LANGUAGES

ITALY: THE FINE ARTS

GERMANY: THE ART OF PAINTING

SPAIN: DISCOVERY

ENGLAND: LITERATURE. The figure is holding a facsimile of the first edition of Shakespeare's *A Midsummer's Night Dream,* printed in 1600.

FRANCE: EMANCIPATION. The figure is holding "Les Droits de l'Homme," The Declaration of the Rights of Man adopted by the French Assembly in 1789.

This photograph of a portion of Edwin H. Blashfield's mural above the Main Reading Room depicts four of the twelve countries, or epochs, that contributed to the "Evolution of Civilization," from Egypt to America.

AMERICA: SCIENCE. The figure, an engineer whose face was modeled from Abraham Lincoln's, sits in his machine shop pondering a problem of mechanics. In front of him is an electric dynamo, representing the American contribution to the advancement of electricity. Blashfield has signed his work on the base of the dynamo, with the accompanying inscription: "These decorations were designed and executed by EDWIN HOWLAND BLASHFIELD, assisted by ARTHUR REGINALD WILLETT, A.D. MDCCCLXXXXVI."

Charles Sprague Pearce painted the two figures and scroll above the window at the west end of the North Mosaic Corridor.

THE NORTH CORRIDOR—FIRST FLOOR

Family and *Education* are major themes in this corridor, which is located behind the north staircase in the Great Hall.

Above the window at the west end of the corridor (through which you can see the Capitol) is a lunette with two female figures holding aloft a scroll with the quotation:

GIVE INSTRUCTION UNTO THOSE WHO CANNOT PROCURE IT FOR THEMSELVES.
Confucius, Book XIII, Section 9

Dominating the corridor are seven paintings by Charles Sprague Pearce. *The Family* is the subject of the large tympanum at the east end, above the entrance to the Librarian's office. The smaller panels near the ceiling along the north wall represent activities associated with family life. From left to right, they depict *Religion, Labor, Study,* and *Recreation.* The single painting on the south side, opposite the panel of *Recreation,* represents *Rest.*

The penetrations in the vault above the paintings contain the surnames of distinguished men of education throughout the world. On the north side, left to right, they are: FROEBEL, PESTALOZZI, ROUSSEAU, COMENIUS, and ASCHAM.

On the south side, above the columns and arches leading to the Great Hall, they are: HOWE, GALLAUDET, MANN, ARNOLD, and SPENCER.

In the mosaic vaulting of the ceiling, from west to east, are the words ART (above the quotation by Confucius), FAMILY, ASTRONOMY (surrounded, clockwise from the north, by MATHEMATICS, CHEMISTRY, PHYSICS, and GEOLOGY), POETRY (surrounded, clockwise from the north, by SCULPTURE, PAINTING, MUSIC, and ARCHITECTURE), EDUCATION, and SCIENCE (above the painting of *The Family*).

The names of the thirteen men appointed by the President of the United States to the post of Librarian of Congress are inscribed on the east wall beneath the painting of *The Family*. The dates are the terms of office served. The Librarians listed above the line served in the Library of Congress in the Capitol, before the Jefferson Building was constructed:

"The Family," a painting by Charles Sprague Pearce, can be seen at the east end of the North Mosaic Corridor. Six other paintings by Pearce are part of this beautiful and elaborately decorated chamber.

JOHN BECKLEY 1802–1807

PATRICK MAGRUDER 1807–1815

GEORGE WATTERSTON 1815–1829

JOHN SILVA MEEHAN 1829–1861

JOHN G. STEPHENSON 1861–1864

AINSWORTH RAND SPOFFORD 1864–1897

. . . .

JOHN RUSSELL YOUNG 1897–1899

HERBERT PUTNAM 1899–1939

ARCHIBALD MACLEISH 1939–1944

LUTHER HARRIS EVANS 1945–1953

LAWRENCE QUINCY MUMFORD 1954–1974

DANIEL J. BOORSTIN 1975–1987

JAMES HADLEY BILLINGTON 1987

THE NORTHWEST CORRIDOR AND PAVILION—FIRST FLOOR

The Northwest Corridor, leading from the Librarian's Room to the Northwest Pavilion, looks out, to the right, on an interior court. The nine lunettes (one at each end of the corridor and seven along the west wall) depict the *Muses* and were rendered by Edward Simmons, who copyrighted each of his paintings in the lower edge.

According to Greek mythology, the Muses were the goddesses of various departments of Art, Poetry, and Science. Apollo, the god of song, was their father, and Mnemosyne (Memory) their mother. Their names, which appear at the center and top of each lunette by Simmons, are listed below, beginning at the south end of the corridor: Melpomene (Tragedy), Clio (History), Thalia (Comedy and Bucolic Poetry), Euterpe (Lyric Song), Terpsichore (Dancing), Erato (Love Poetry), Polyhymia (Sacred Song), Urania (Astronomy), and Calliope (Epic Poetry).

Three of the paintings have quotations beneath them.

Beneath Thalia:

DESCEND, YE NINE! DESCEND AND SING

WAKE INTO VOICE EACH SILENT STRING

Pope, Ode on St. Cecilia's Day

Beneath Terpsichore:

O HEAV'N-BORN SISTERS! SOURCE OF ART!

WHO CHARM THE SENSE, OR MEND THE HEART.

Pope, Two Choruses to the Tragedy of Brutus

Beneath Urania:

SAY, WILL YE BLESS THE BLEAK ATLANTIC SHORE,

AND IN THE WEST BID ATHENS RISE ONCE MORE?

Pope, Two Choruses to the Tragedy of Brutus

The Northwest Pavilion at the end of the corridor is decorated with medallions containing figures of dancing girls by Robert Leftwich Dodge. A series of the signs of the zodiac, designed by W. Mills Thompson, is in the six arched windows.

THE LIBRARIAN'S ROOM
(VISITED ONLY BY PERMISSION)

Now used primarily for ceremonial purposes, this room was the office of the Librarian of Congress from 1897 until 1980, when the office was moved to the Madison Building.

The central disc of the domed ceiling contains a painting by Edward J. Holslag, representing Letters. The following sentence is inscribed on a streamer:

LITERA SCRIPTA MANET [The written word endures]

There are four additional circular paintings in the pendentives (corners) of the dome, signed, like the dome painting, "E. J. Holslag." The inscriptions, starting over the door and moving left to right, read as follows:

IN TENEBRIS LUX [In darkness light]

LIBER DILECTATIO ANIMAE [Books, the delight of the soul]

EFFICIUNT CLARUM STUDIO [They make it clear by study]

DULCE ANTE OMNIA MUSAE [The Muses, above all things, delightful]

Henry Oliver Walker's mural "Lyric Poetry," is at the east end of the South Mosaic Corridor, a hallway that celebrates both European and American poets. The Americans are: Ralph Waldo Emerson, Henry Wadsworth Longfellow, James Russell Lowell, John Greenleaf Whittier, William Cullen Bryant, Walt Whitman, and Edgar Allan Poe.

Lyric Poetry is the decoration theme in the corridor behind the south staircase in the Great Hall.

Above the window at the west end (through which you can see the Capitol and, beyond that, the Mall), a broad border contains an idyllic summer landscape. At the top is a banner with a quotation from Wordsworth:

THE POETS, WHO ON EARTH HAVE MADE US HEIRS
OF TRUTH AND PURE DELIGHT BY HEAVENLY LAYS.

Henry Oliver Walker's mural *Lyric Poetry*—found at the east end of the corridor—provides the general theme. Lyric Poetry stands with a lyre in the center; the words "Lyric Poetry" can be seen in the lunette border directly above her. Other figures, seen from left to right, are Mirth (boy), Beauty (seated woman), Passion (woman with right arm held high), Pathos (woman standing upward), Truth (standing nude), and Devotion (seated woman).

The names of fifteen Library of Congress employees who died in World War II are inscribed on a marble panel beneath the mural.

Henry Oliver Walker also painted the smaller lunettes along the south and north walls. In each, Walker depicts a youth suggested by the work of an American or an English poet.

The poets represented on the panels on the south wall and the poem represented by the figure in the lunette are, from east to west:

Tennyson

The panel refers to these lines from the poem, "Palace of Art":

FLUSHED GANYMEDE, HIS ROSY THIGH
HALF-BURIED IN THE EAGLE'S DOWN,
SOLE AS A FLYING STAR SHOT THRO' THE SKY
ABOVE THE PILLAR'D TOWN

Keats

The panel represents Endymion, in Keats' poem of that name.

Wordsworth

The panel is based on Wordsworth's lines beginning:

THERE WAS A BOY; YE KNEW HIM WELL, YE CLIFFS
AND ISLANDS OF WINANDER!

Emerson

The panel is based on Emerson's lines from "Uriel:"

LINE IN A NATURE IS NOT FOUND
UNIT AND UNIVERSE ARE ROUND;
IN VAIN PRODUCED, ALL RAYS RETURN
EVIL WILL BLESS, AND ICE WILL BURN

Alfred Tennyson's poem "Ganymede" is one of six poems depicted in paintings by Henry Oliver Walker in the South Mosaic Corridor. The most famous poet of the Victorian age, Tennyson is well-represented throughout the Jefferson Building; his name is in the ceiling of the Great Hall, and his poetry is also found in the Southwest Corridor on the first floor (The Greek Heroes) and the Great Hall's second floor North Corridor.

The poets represented on the panels along the north wall and the lines referred to are, from east to west:

Milton

The panel is based on Milton's poem "Comus":
CAN ANY MORTAL MIXTURE OF EARTH'S MOULD
BREATH SUCH DIVINE ENCHANTING RAVISHMENT?

Shakespeare

The panel refers to the poem *Venus and Adonis,* showing
the body of Adonis, killed by the boar.

The names of lyric poets are contained in the mosaic of the ceiling vault. Six Americans are honored on the north side: LONGFELLOW, LOWELL, WHITTIER, BRYANT, WHITMAN, and POE. Poets honored on the south side are the Europeans HEINE, HUGO, MUSSET, BYRON, SHELLEY, and BROWNING. The names of ancient poets are inscribed in the center of the vault: THEOCRITUS, PINDAR, ANACREON, SAPPHO, CATULLUS, HORACE, PETRARCH, and RONSARD.

THE SOUTHWEST CORRIDOR—FIRST FLOOR

The Southwest Corridor—leading from the South Mosaic Corridor *(Lyric Poetry)* to the Southwest Pavilion—looks out, to the left, on an interior court. The nine lunettes (one at each end of the corridor and seven along the west wall) contain paintings by Walter McEwen which represent *The Greek Heroes* (note the artist's copyright notice on each lunettte). Beginning over the doorway at the north end, continuing along the west wall, and ending at the south end, the paintings depict Paris, Jason, Bellerophon, Orpheus, Perseus, Prometheus, Theseus, Achilles, and Hercules. The name of each Greek hero can be seen at the top center of each border. Four of the paintings have quotations beneath them.

Beneath *Jason:*
ONE EQUAL TEMPER OF HEROIC HEARTS,
MADE WEAK BY TIME AND FATE, BUT STRONG IN WILL
TO STRIVE, TO SEEK, TO FIND, AND NOT TO YIELD
Tennyson, Ulysses

Beneath *Orpheus:*

A GLORIOUS COMPANY, THE FLOWER OF MEN,
TO SERVE AS MODEL FOR THE MIGHTY WORLD,
AND BE THE FAIR BEGINNING OF A TIME

Tennyson, Idylls of the King

Beneath *Prometheus:*

TO THE SOULS OF FIRE, I, PALLAS ATHENA, GIVE MORE FIRE,
AND TO THOSE WHO ARE MANFUL, A MIGHT MORE THAN A MAN'S.

Charles Kingsley, The Heroes: Perseus

Beneath *Achilles:*

ANCIENT OF DAYS! AUGUST ATHENA! WHERE,
WHERE ARE THY MEN OF MIGHT, THY GRAND IN SOUL?
GONE GLIMMERING THROUGH THE DREAM OF THINGS THAT WERE

Byron, Childe Harold

THE MEMBERS OF CONGRESS READING ROOM
(VISITED ONLY BY PERMISSION)

Now used by all Members of Congress and their staffs, this richly decorated gallery was reserved for Members of the House of Representatives when the Jefferson Building opened in 1897.

Along the center of the ceiling are panels by Carl Gutherz that represent civilization through the Spectrum of Light. Each of the seven panels, unfortunately rather pale (though the artist's copyright notices are still legible), features a central figure who symbolizes some phase of achievement, human or divine. The cherubs in the corners of each panel represent the arts or sciences, and the escutcheons in each panel present the title of the decoration, the seals of the various states of the nation, and the mottoes of those seals. (Several of the seals do not have mottoes and the seals of California, Minnesota, and South Dakota are omitted altogether.)

The order of the subjects begins with the central panel (Yellow: "Let There Be Light") and moves south (Orange, Red, Violet) and then north (Green, Blue, Indigo) from the center. The several hues of the spectrum are separately diffused over each panel, decreasing in intensity as they recede from the central figures.

Let There Be Light (Yellow)

The subject is the creation of light. The Divine Intelligence, sitting enthroned in the midst of space, utters the words, "Let there be light." (Holy Bible, Genesis: 1:3) The cherubs in the corners represent Physics, Metaphysics, Psychology, and Theology.

FINIS CORONAT OPUS [The end crowns the work]

GLORIA VIRTUTIS UMBRA [Glory the shadow of virtue]
Cicero: Tusc. Disputationum, *i. 45*

Massachusetts
ENSE PETIT PLACIDAM SUB LIBERATE QUIETUM [Peace under Liberty]

Kentucky
UNITED WE STAND; DIVIDED WE FALL
*Morris (quoted in "The Flag of Our Country Forever,"
from* The Liberty Tree *by John Dickinson)*

South Carolina
ANIMUS OPIBUSQUE PARATI [Prepared in mind and resources]
Virgil, Aeneid, *ii, 799*

DUM SPIRO SPERO [While I breathe, I hope]

The Light of Excellence (Orange)

The subject of excellence was suggested to the artist by Longfellow's poem, *Excelsior.* A spirit on a pyramid of steps (signifying Progress) holds a streamer bearing the mottoes: COURAGE, EFFORT, EXCELLENCE, EXCELSIOR. The corner cherubs typify phases of human development regarding Architecture and Art; Transportation; the Phonograph and Telephone; and Invention and Design.

Georgia
CONSTITUTION! WISDOM. JUSTICE. MODERATION.

New York
EXCELSIOR [Higher]

Delaware
LIBERTY AND INDEPENDENCE

New Hampshire

Connecticut

QUI TRANSTULIT SUSTINET [Who transplanted sustains]

Rhode Island

HOPE

Vermont

FREEDOM AND UNITY

The Light of Poetry (Red)

The genius of Poetry, mounted upon Pegasus, soars aloft. The corner cherubs stand for Tragedy and Comedy; Lyric Poetry; Pastoral Poetry; and Fable.

Alabama

HERE WE REST

Tennessee

AGRICULTURE, COMMERCE

Arkansas

REGNANT POPULI [The people rule]

MERCY! JUSTICE!

Florida

IN GOD WE TRUST

Michigan

SI QUAERIS PENINSULAM AMOENAM, CIRCUMSPICE
[If thou seekest a beautiful peninsula, behold it here]
TUEBOR [I will defend]
E PLURIBUS UNUM [From one, many]

North Carolina

ESSE QUAM VIDERI [To be, rather than to seem]

Sallust

CONSTITUTION

Louisiana

UNION. JUSTICE. CONFIDENCE.

The Light of State (Violet)

America, or Columbia, supports the shield of the United States; her liberty cap is inscribed "1776." The color was chosen by the artist because violet results from the union of the American colors red, white, and blue. The cherubs in the corners represent Suffrage, Justice, Liberty, and Equality.

Washington, D.C.
JUSTITIA OMNIBUS [Justice for all]

Montana
ORO Y PLATA [Gold and silver]

Iowa
OUR LIBERTIES WE PRIZE, AND OUR RIGHTS WE WILL MAINTAIN

Texas

Maryland
FATTI MASCHII; PAROLE FEMINE [Manly deeds; womanly words]
SCUTO BONAE VOLUNTATIS TUAE CORONASTI NOS
[Thy good will is our shield]

Virginia
SIC SEMPER TYRANNIS [Thus ever to tyrants]

Pennsylvania
VIRTUE, LIBERTY, AND INDEPENDENCE

The Light of Research (Green)

The central figure is the Spirit of the Lens, which through the telescope and microscope reveals the secrets of the universe. The cherubs represent original investigation and research, specifically in Chemistry, Archeology (Egyptology deciphering the hieroglyphics); and Mineralogy.

Nebraska
EQUALITY BEFORE THE LAW

Utah
INDUSTRY

Wisconsin
FORWARD! E PLURIBUS UNUM [From one, many]

Nevada
ALL FOR OUR COUNTRY

Missouri
SALUS POPULI SUPREMA LEX ESTO
[Let the safety of people be the supreme law]
Cicero, The Twelve Tables

UNITED WE STAND; DIVIDED WE FALL
Morris

Indiana

Illinois
STATE SOVEREIGNTY. NATIONAL UNION

The Light of Truth (Blue)
The Spirit of Truth tramples the Dragon of Ignorance and Falsehood and reaches to heaven for a ray of light with which to inflict the final wound. The cherubs hold the level, the plumb, the square, and the Bible, each considered an agent in the presence of Universal Law.

Wyoming
EQUAL RIGHTS

Idaho
ESTO PERPETUA [Let it endure forever].

Arizona
DITAT DEUS [God enriches]

North Dakota
LIBERTY AND UNION, NOW AND FOREVER, ONE AND INSEPARABLE!
Webster, Second Speech on Foot's Resolution, *January 26, 1830*

New Mexico
CRESCIT EUNDO [Ever stronger and stronger]
Virgil, Aeneid

Colorado
NIL SINE NUMINE [Nothing without God]

West Virginia
MONTANI SEMPER LIBERI [Mountaineers are always freemen]

The Light of Science (Indigo)

Science is represented in the figure of Astronomy, who is guided by the soul (represented by a butterfly fluttering above her head) to explore the movement of the heavens. The cherubs represent various phases of astronomical study.

New Jersey
LIBERTY AND PROSPERITY

Washington

Oregon
THE UNION

Ohio

Kansas
AD ASTRA PER ASPERA [To the stars through difficulties]
Seneca

Mississippi

Maine
DIRIGO [I direct]

Large mosaic panels by Frederick Dielman, signed and copyrighted, are displayed over the marble fireplaces at each end of the room: Law, at the north, History at the south. In Law the names of the figures INDUSTRY, PEACE, and TRUTH, the friends and supporters of the Law, can be seen on the left side; on the other side of the throne are FRAUD, DISCORD, and VIOLENCE, Law's enemies. In History, the names of the figures MYTHOLOGY and TRADITION, the predecessors of History, can be seen. On either side of the central figure are inscribed the names of great historians: HERODOTUS, THUCYDIDES, POLYBIUS, LIVY, TACITUS, BAEDA, COMINES, HUME, GIBBON, NIEBUHR, GUIZOT, RANKE, BANCROFT, and MOTLEY.

Now used by the Library's Council of Scholars, the Southwest Pavilion was originally reserved for use by Members of the Senate. It is entered through a small marble-panelled lobby at the end of the southwest corridor. In his *Handbook,* Herbert Small called this lobby "one of the most beautiful examples of pure architecture design" to be found in the Library. Small found the whole effect of the lobby's decoration "remarkably fine—a combination of great richness with soberness and refinement."

The lunette over the entrance contains a curved panel by Herbert Adams, with a heraldic wooden shield bearing the monogram "USA." The gold ceiling paintings consist of six square panels by the artist William A. MacKay. In the southwest corner of the pavilion is a fireplace made of Siena marble. Above the fireplace is a sculptured panel by Herbert Adams, the design of which shows an eagle with arrows in its claws and an American shield supported by flying cherubs. The relief is signed, and on the banner beneath the shield is the motto E PLURIBUS UNUM (From one, many).

THE GREAT HALL—SECOND FLOOR

The East Corridor

In the center of the ceiling vault are three panels by William A. MacKay which represent the Life of Man. On either side of these panels are the following quotations that refer to this monumental subject.

They are, on the west side (or at the head of the paintings), from left to right:

COMES THE BLIND FURY WITH THE ABHORRED SHEARS
AND SLITS THE THIN-SPUN LIFE
Milton, Lycidas, *75*

THE WEB OF LIFE IS OF A MINGLED YARN, GOOD AND ILL TOGETHER
Shakespeare, All's Well That Ends Well, *Act iv., Scene 2*

FOR A WEB BEGUN GOD SENDS THREAD
Old Proverb

Frederick Dielman's large mosaic panel "Law" is above the fireplace at the north end of the Members of Congress Reading Room. The friends of Law (Industry, Peace, and Truth) are on the left; its enemies (Fraud, Discord, and Violence) are on the other side of the throne.

Dielman's mosaic "History," above the fireplace at the south end of the room, depicts the predecessors of history (Mythology and Tradition) and lists the names of fourteen great historians including one American, George Bancroft.

The quotations on the east, or at the foot of the central vault paintings, are taken from Cardinal Wolsey's speech in Shakespeare's *Henry VIII*. From left to right, they are:

THIS IS THE STATE OF MAN: TO-DAY HE PUTS FORTH
THE TENDER LEAVES OF HOPE.
TO-MORROW BLOSSOMS
AND BEARS HIS BLUSHING HONORS THICK UPON HIM.
THE THIRD DAY COMES A FROST,
AND NIPS HIS ROOT,
AND THEN HE FALLS.
Act iii, Scene 2

On either side of these panels are four rectangular paintings by George Randolph Barse, Jr., representing *Literature*. Along the east side, beginning at the north, are LYRICA (Lyric Poetry), TRAGEDY, COMEDY, and HISTORY. On the west side, again beginning at the south, are ROMANCE, FANCY, TRADITION, and EROTICA (Love Poetry).

At each end of the ceiling vault is a tablet containing the surnames of eminent American printers, and men who have contributed to the improvement of American printing machinery. At the north end are the names of GREEN, DAYE, FRANKLIN, THOMAS, and BRADFORD; at the south end, the names are CLYMER, ADAMS, GORDON, HOE, and BRUCE.

The quotations on the gilt wall tablets above the windows along the east side are:

SCIENCE IS ORGANIZED KNOWLEDGE
Herbert Spencer, Essays, *"The Genesis of Science," Volume ii, 1.*

Around the corner, facing the staircase, you will find:
BEAUTY IS TRUTH, TRUTH BEAUTY
Keats, Ode on a Grecian Urn

On the other side of the staircase:
TOO LOW THEY BUILD WHO BUILD BENEATH THE STARS
Edward Young, Night Thoughts, *"Night," viii, 215*

And around the corner, facing the Great Hall:
THERE IS BUT ONE TEMPLE IN THE UNIVERSE
AND THAT IS THE BODY OF MAN
Novalis, Philosophy and Physics

Printers' marks, or trade marks from printers and publishers, embellish the upper walls of all four corridors on the second floor of the Great Hall. In the east corridor the following marks can be found:

Along the north wall:

L. DE GIUNTA, ALDUS MANUTIUS

Along the east wall, beginning on the left:

P. AND A. MEIETOS, G. DI LEGNANO, J. ROSEMBACH,
A. TORRESANO, V. FERNANDEZ

Along the south wall:

C. PLANTIN, I. ELZEVIR

Along the west wall, beginning on the left:

FRATRES DE SABIO, MELCHIOR SESSA, O. SCOTTO,
GIAM. RIZZARDI, F DE GIUNTA

The Entrance to the Visitors' Gallery, Main Reading Room

The vaulting of the passageway leading to the Visitors' Gallery consists of a series of six small domes. In the medallions are various objects symbolizing the Fine Arts, specifically Acting, Music, Sculpture, Literature, and Architecture.

The trophies of Sculpture and Architecture are accompanied by appropriate names. The subjects of the sculptures are the Farnese Bull, the Laocoon, the Niobe, and the Parthenon pediment. In the bordering arabesques are the names of the four divinities often taken as the subject of ancient statuary: VENUS, APOLLO, HERCULES, and ZEUS. For Architecture, the buildings commemorated are the COLOSSEUM, the TAJ MAHAL, the PARTHENON, and the PYRAMIDS, and the cities are those with whose fame these monuments are connected: ROME, AGRA, ATHENS, and GIZEH.

In the bays opposite the two elevator entrances are two small lunettes. The painting on the north side depicts John James Audubon, the one on the south, the historian William Hickling Prescott, with Prescott's name on the painting. These two paintings, by an unknown artist, replaced the original paintings, "L'Allegro" and "Il Penseroso" by William G. Van Ingen, sometime between the opening of the building in 1897 and 1911. The Van Ingen paintings, according to Small's *Handbook,* "suggested the subjects of Milton's well-known companion poems" and included inscriptions of portions of the two poems.

Minerva

A marble mosaic of Minerva by Elihu Vedder can be seen along the wall of the staircase landing that leads to the Visitors' Gallery. The artist's name can be seen beneath the owl near her right foot. Her armor partly laid aside, this Minerva of Peace is depicted as the vigilant guardian of civilization. The various fields of learning, listed on a scroll in Minerva's hand, are: AGRICULTURE, EDUCATION, MECHANICS, COMMERCE, GOVERNMENT, HISTORY, ASTRONOMY, GEOGRAPHY, STATISTICS, ECONOMICS, PAINTING, SCULPTURE, ARCHITECTURE, MUSIC, POETRY, BIOGRAPHY, GEOLOGY, BOTANY, MEDICINE, PHILOSOPHY, LAW, POLITICS, ARBITRATION, TREATIES, ARMY-NAVY, FINANCE, ART OF WAR.

Beneath the mosaic is the inscription:

NIL INVITA MINERVA QUAE MONUMENTUM AERE PERENNIUS EXEGIT
[Not unwilling, Minerva raises a monument more lasting than bronze]
Horace, Ars Poetica, *385; Carminum, iii, 30, 1.*

The South Corridor

Frank Weston Benson's paintings dominate the south wall and the ceiling. The subject of Benson's four circular panels on the south wall is the Seasons, each represented by a half-length figure of a young woman. From east to west, beginning above the first door leading into the Southwest Gallery, they are Spring, Summer, Autumn, and Winter. In the ceiling vault, the *Three Graces* are depicted in octagonal panels, from east to west: Aglaia (Husbandry), Thalia (Music), and Euphrosyne (Beauty). At each end of the ceiling is a rectangular panel by Frederic C. Martin painted in a style depicting ancient games, but representing the modern sports of football (east end) and baseball (west end).

At the west end, Pompeiian panels by George Maynard of PRUDENCE and TEMPERANCE flank the window, just as on the east side Maynard has depicted PATRIOTISM and COURAGE. The bas-reliefs in the vault, above the west window, are by Roland Hinton Perry, and represent the *Sibyls,* or ancient prophetesses, who interpreted omens, delivered oracles, and foretold the future. The sibyls here portrayed are the Cumaean or Roman Sibyl (first panel) and, on the other side of the arch, a Scandinavian Vala or Wise Woman.

Around the west end window (through which you can see the Capitol), there are five semicircular or circular tablets, two of which are ornamented with the obverse and reverse of the Great Seal of the United States. The other three carry the following quotations:

BENEATH THE RULE OF MEN ENTIRELY GREAT,
THE PEN IS MIGHTIER THAN THE SWORD
Bulwer Lytton, Richelieu: *Act ii., Scene 2*

A quotation from Sir Philip Sidney accompanies Frank W. Benson's painting "Summer" in the South Corridor ceiling in the Great Hall. The decorations surrounding the panel—and throughout the building—were the responsibility of Elmer E. Garnsey, who also supervised the lettering of the inscriptions and quotations.

THEY ARE NEVER ALONE
THAT ARE ACCOMPANIED
WITH NOBLE THOVGHTS.

MAN RAISES, BUT TIME WEIGHS
Modern Greek Proverb

THE NOBLEST MOTIVE IS THE PUBLIC GOOD
Virgil

Quotations on the gilt tablets, beginning under the window on the east end and moving to the right, from east to west along the south wall are:

BEHOLDING THE BRIGHT COUNTENANCE OF TRUTH, IN THE QUIET
AND STILL AIR OF DELIGHTFUL STUDIES.
Milton, Introduction to Church Government

THE TRUE UNIVERSITY OF THESE DAYS IS A COLLECTION OF BOOKS
Carlyle, On Heroes and Hero-Worship
"The Hero as a Man of Letters"

NATURE IS THE ART OF GOD
Sir Thomas Browne

THERE IS NO WORK OF GENIUS WHICH HAS NOT BEEN
THE DELIGHT OF MANKIND
Lowell, Among My Books

IT IS THE MIND THAT MAKES THE MAN, AND OUR VIGOR
IS IN OUR IMMORTAL SOUL
Ovid

THEY ARE NEVER ALONE THAT ARE ACCOMPANIED WITH NOBLE THOUGHTS
Sir Philip Sidney, Arcadia

MAN IS ONE WORLD AND HATH ANOTHER TO ATTEND HIM
Herbert, The Temple

TONGUES IN TREES, BOOKS IN THE RUNNING BROOKS, SERMONS IN STONES,
AND GOOD IN EVERYTHING
Shakespeare, As You Like It, *Act ii, Scene 1*

THE TRUE SHEKINAH IS MAN
St. John Chrysostom

The "Tongues in Trees" quotation accompanying this Frank W. Benson painting of "Winter" is from William Shakespeare's play, "As You Like It." Shakespeare is the best represented writer in the Jefferson Building's iconography; his name is in the Great Hall ceiling, his bronze statue in the Main Reading Room, and words from his poetry and plays are in the first floor Southwest Corridor (Lyric Poetry) and the second-floor East, South, and North Corridors.

TONGVES IN TREES BOOKS IN THE
RVNNING BROOKS SERMONS IN STONES
AND GOOD IN EVERYTHING.

And above the west window:

ONLY THE ACTIONS OF THE JUST SMELL SWEET AND BLOSSOM IN THE DUST
Shirley, Contention of Ajax and Ulysses, *Scene 2.*

Quotations on the wall above the golden tablets, beginning between the windows on the west end and moving to the right along the north wall, are:

A LITTLE LEARNING IS A DANGEROUS THING;
DRINK DEEP OR TASTE NOT OF THE PIERIAN SPRING.
Pope, Essay on Criticism, *Part ii, 215*

LEARNING IS BUT AN ADJUNCT TO OURSELF
Shakespeare, Love's Labor Lost, *Act iv., Scene 3*

STUDIES PERFECT NATURE AND ARE PERFECTED BY EXPERIENCE
Bacon, Essays, *"Of Studies"*

DREAMS, BOOKS, ARE EACH A WORLD; BOOKS WE KNOW,
ARE A SUBSTANTIAL WORLD, BOTH PURE AND GOOD
Wordsworth, Personal Talk, *Sonnet iii*

THE FAULT IS NOT IN OUR STARS
BUT IN OURSELVES, THAT WE ARE UNDERLINGS
Shakespeare, Julius Caesar, *Act 1, Scene 2*

THE UNIVERSAL CAUSE
ACTS TO ONE END, BUT ACTS BY VARIOUS LAWS
Pope, Essay on Man, *Epistle iii, 1*

CREATION'S HEIR, THE WORLD, THE WORLD IS MINE!
Goldsmith, The Traveller, *50*

VAIN, VERY VAIN, THE WEARY SEARCH TO FIND
THAT BLISS WHICH ONLY CENTRES IN THE MIND
Goldsmith, The Traveller, *423*

Medallions representing different fields of knowledge and endeavor are interspersed with the quotations, paintings, and printers' marks. On the south wall, from east to west, are PRINTING, POTTERY, and GLASS-MAKING; on the north wall, from west to east, are CARPENTRY, SMITHERY, and MASONRY.

Printers' marks, or trade marks from printers and publishers, embellish the south and north walls. On the south wall, from east to west, the marks are for:

On the north wall, from west to east, the marks are for:

WÉCHEL; TORY; CHAUDIÈRE; LE ROUGE; BREUILLE; DOLET; TRESCHEL; PETIT

The West Corridor

In the center of the ceiling vault are three panels by William B. Van Ingren representing Painting, Architecture, and Sculpture. On either side of these medallions are four rectangular paintings by Walter Shirlaw, representing The Sciences. Along the west side, beginning at the left, are ZOOLOGY, PHYSICS, MATHEMATICS, and GEOLOGY. On the east, again beginning at the left, are ARCHAEOLOGY, BOTANY, ASTRONOMY, and CHEMISTRY.

At either end of the vault is a tablet containing the names of scientists. At the north end are: LA GRANGE, LAVOISIER, RUMFORD, and LYELL; at the south end are: CUVIER, LINNAEUS, SCHLIEMANN, and COPERNICUS. On either side of these tablets, are these quotations:

South tablet:

THE FIRST CREATURE OF GOD WAS THE LIGHT OF SENSE;
THE LAST WAS THE LIGHT OF REASON
Bacon, Essays, *"Of Truth"*

THE LIGHT SHINETH IN DARKNESS, AND THE DARKNESS
COMPREHENDED NOT
Holy Bible, John 1:5

North tablet:

ALL ARE BUT PARTS OF ONE STUPENDOUS WHOLE,
WHOSE BODY NATURE IS, AND GOD THE SOUL
Pope, Essay on Man, *"Epistle" i, 267*

IN NATURE ALL IS USEFUL, ALL IS BEAUTIFUL
Emerson, Essays, *"Art"*

Quotations on the gilt wall tablets along the west side, beginning at the left, are as follows:

ART IS LONG, AND TIME IS FLEETING
Longfellow, A Psalm of Life

THE HISTORY OF THE WORLD IS THE BIOGRAPHY OF GREAT MEN

Carlyle, Essays, *"History"*

BOOKS WILL SPEAK PLAIN WHEN COUNSELLORS BLANCH

Bacon, Essays, *"Of Counsel"*

GLORY IS ACQUIRED BY VIRTUE BUT PRESERVED BY LETTERS

Petrarch

THE FOUNDATION OF EVERY STATE IS THE EDUCATION OF ITS YOUTH

Dionysius

Printers' marks or trade marks from printers and publishers embellish the east and west walls. Along the east wall, beginning at the upper left, the marks are for these firms:

CRATANDER; VALENTIN KOBIAN; MARTIN SCHOTT; MELCHIOR LOTTER; T. and J. RIHEL

Along the west wall, beginning on the left, the marks are for:

WOLFANG KOPFEL, FUST AND SCHOEFFER, CRAFT MULLER, CONRAD BAUMGARTIN, JACOB DE PFORTZEM

The North Corridor

Robert Reid's brilliantly colored paintings dominate the north wall and the ceiling. Reid's four circular panels on the north wall, from west to east, are titled WISDOM, UNDERSTANDING, KNOWLEDGE, and PHILOSOPHY. In the ceiling vault, the octagonal decorations represent the five senses: TASTE, SIGHT, SMELL, HEARING, and TOUCH. Alternating with the ceiling paintings are a series of rectangular panels by Frederic C. Martin that depict events in ancient sports. The scenes, from west to east in the ceiling, are of discus throwing, wrestling, running, the rub-down, victory, and the return home.

At the west end, Pompeiian panels depicting INDUSTRY and CONCORDIA by George Maynard flank the window, just as on the east side Maynard has pictured FORTITUDE and JUSTICE. The bas-reliefs in the vault above the west window are by Roland Hinton Perry. They represent the Sibyls, ancient prophetesses who interpreted omens, delivered oracles, and foretold the future. The sibyls portrayed here are the Greek Sybil and the Eastern, or Persian Sybil. In the first panel, the Greek Sybil is represented by the priestess of the world-renowned Oracle at Delphi. In the second panel, the face of the prophetess is veiled, signifying the occult wisdom of the East.

Above the west window is the quotation:

THE CHIEF GLORY OF EVERY PEOPLE ARISES FROM ITS AUTHORS
Johnson, Preface, A Dictionary of the English Language

Around the west window are five round tablets, two of which are ornamented with the obverse and reserve of the Great Seal of the United States. The other three carry the following quotations:

ORDER IS HEAVEN'S FIRST LAW
Pope, Essay on Man, *"Epistle," iv., 49*

MEMORY IS THE TREASURER AND GUARDIAN OF ALL THINGS
Cicero, De Oratore, *i., 5*

BEAUTY IS THE CREATOR OF THE UNIVERSE
Emerson, Essays, *"The Poet"*

Quotations on the golden wall tablets on the north wall, from west to east, are:

THERE IS ONE ONLY GOOD, NAMELY, KNOWLEDGE;
AND ONE ONLY EVIL, NAMELY IGNORANCE
Diogenes Laertius, Socrates, *Section xiv.*

KNOWLEDGE COMES, BUT WISDOM LINGERS
Tennyson, Locksley Hall, *Stanza 72*

WISDOM IS THE PRINCIPAL THING; THEREFORE GET WISDOM;
AND WITH ALL THY GETTING, GET UNDERSTANDING
Holy Bible, Proverbs 4:7

IGNORANCE IS THE CURSE OF GOD,
KNOWLEDGE THE WING WHEREWITH WE FLY TO HEAVEN
Shakespeare, Henry IV, *pt. ii, Act iv., Scene 7*

HOW CHARMING IS DIVINE PHILOSOPHY!
Milton, Comus, *476*

BOOKS MUST FOLLOW SCIENCES, AND NOT SCIENCES BOOKS
Bacon, Proposition Touching Amendment of Laws

IN BOOKS LIES THE SOUL OF THE WHOLE PAST TIME

Carlyle, On Heroes and Hero-Worship, *"The Hero as a Man of Letters"*

WORDS ARE ALSO ACTIONS AND ACTIONS ARE A KIND OF WORDS

Emerson, Essays, *"The Poet"*

Between the windows on the golden tablet at the east end of the corridor is the quotation:

READING MAKETH A FULL MAN; CONFERENCE A READY MAN;
AND WRITING, AN EXACT MAN

Bacon, Essays, *"Of Studies"*

Excerpts from "Unexpressed," a poem by Adelaide Procter, are found on seven tablets on the north and south walls. On the south wall, reading from left to right, the verses are:

NO REAL POET EVER WOVE IN NUMBERS
ALL HIS DREAMS
LOVE AND LIFE UNITED
ARE TWIN MYSTERIES, DIFFERENT YET THE SAME
LOVE MAY STRIVE, BUT VAIN IS THE ENDEAVOR
ALL ITS BOUNDLESS RICHES TO EXPRESS
ART AND LOVE SPEAK AND THEIR WORDS MUST BE
LIKE SIGHINGS OF ILLIMITABLE FORESTS

On the north wall:

DWELLS WITHIN THE SOUL OF EVERY ARTIST
MORE THAN ALL HIS EFFORT CAN EXPRESS
NO GREAT THINKER EVER LIVED AND TAUGHT YOU
ALL THE WONDER THAT HIS SOUL RECEIVED
NO TRUE PAINTER SET ON CANVAS
ALL THE GLORIOUS VISION HE CONCEIVED
NO MUSICIAN
BUT BE SURE HE HEARD, AND STROVE TO RENDER,
FEEBLE ECHOES OF CELESTIAL STRAINS

Interspersed with the quotations from the poem "Unexpressed" are medallions representing different fields of knowledge and endeavor. On the south wall, from east to west, are NAVIGATION, MECHANICS, and TRANSPORATION; on the north wall, from west to east, are GEOMETRY, METEOROLOGY, and FORESTRY.

Printers' marks, or trade marks from printers and publishers, embellish the north and south walls. On the south wall, from east to west, the marks are for:

WILLIAM CAXTON; R. GRAFTON; VAUTROLLIER; JOHN DAY; W. JAGGARD; AR-BUTHNOT; A. HESTER; R. PYNSON.

On the north wall, from west to east, the marks are for these firms:

D. APPLETON AND CO.; THE DEVINNE PRESS; CHARLES SCRIBNER'S SONS; HARPER AND BROTHERS; THE RIVERSIDE PRESS; THE CENTURY CO.; J.B. LIP-PINCOTT CO.; DODD MEAD AND CO.

THE SECOND FLOOR GALLERIES AND PAVILIONS

The Southwest Gallery (The Arts and the Sciences)

The paintings in the large lunettes at each end of the Southwest Gallery are by Kenyon Cox: *The Sciences* at the south end, and *The Arts* at the north end of the gallery.

Names of renowned artists and scientists are inscribed on tablets above the windows and the doors. Starting at the north entrance near *The Arts* and moving south, they are: WAGNER, HOMER, MICHELANGELO, RAPHAEL, RUBENS, MILTON, LEIBNITZ, DALTON, KEPLER, HERSCHEL, GALILEO, ARISTOTLE, PTOLEMY, HIPPARCHUS, LAMARCK, HELMHOLTZ, PHIDIAS, VITRUVIUS, BRA-MANTE, and MOZART.

The monogram "CL" for Congressional Library is used as a decorative feature in the ceiling.

The Southwest Pavilion (The Discoverers)

The paintings in the lunettes and the disc in the domed ceiling are the work of George Willoughby Maynard. In the lunettes the sequence of Maynard's subjects begins on the east side and continues to the right, as follows: AD-VENTURE, DISCOVERY, CONQUEST, CIVILIZATION. In the ceiling disc, the artist has depicted four qualities appropriate to these four stages of a country's development: COURAGE, VALOR, FORTITUDE, and ACHIEVEMENT.

The paintings in the lunettes include the names of illustrious discoverers and adventurers. They are, as follows:

East Lunette (Adventure):

DRAKE	DIAZ
CAVENDISH	NARVAEZ
RALEIGH	COELHO
SMITH	CABEZA
FROBISHER	VERRAZANO
GILBERT	BASTIDAS

South Lunette (Discovery):

SOLIS	CABOT
ORELLANA	MAGELLAN
VAN HORN	HUDSON
OIEDA	BEHRING
COLUMBUS	VESPUCIUS
PINZON	BALBOA

West Lunette (Conquest)

PIZARRO	CORTES
ALVARADO	STANDISH
ALMAGRO	WINSLOW
HUTTEN	PHIPS
FRONTENAC	VELASQUEZ
DE SOTO	DE LEON

North Lunette (Civilization)

ELIOT	PENN
CALVERT	WINTHROP
MARQUETTE	MOTOLINIA
JOLIET	FRITZ
OGLETHORPE	YEARDLEY
LAS CASAS	LA SALLE

This construction photograph shows ornaments being prepared for installation in the second floor gallery ceilings. The "CL" stands for "Congressional Library," the name by which the Library of Congress was known at the turn of the century. The gilding of the rosettes (foreground) was another responsibility of Elmer E. Garnsey, who also supervised the setting of tiles, the assembling of the mosaics, the color coordination, and the execution of the painted panels.

The wall tablets bear these words, beginning in the southwest corner and proceeding to the right:

ARTS, LETTERS, TOLERATION, SPAIN, ENTERPRISE, OPPORTUNITY, FORTUNE, PORTUGAL, INDIA, ELDORADO, AMERICA, FRANCE, EXPLORATION, DOMINION, COLONIZATION, ENGLAND

Circular plaques in relief, representing the Four Seasons, are in the four corners beneath the ceiling. The series, repeated in the other three second floor pavilions, is the work of Bela Lyon Pratt. Beginning in the corner and

proceeding clockwise, *Spring* carries the label *Seed, Summer* is *Bloom, Autumn* is *Fruit,* and *Winter* is *Decay.*

The Northwest Gallery (War and Peace)

The paintings in the large lunettes at each end of the Northwest Gallery are by Gari Melchers: *Peace* at the south end, and *War* at the north end of the gallery. Names of famous generals and admirals are on tablets above the windows and doors. Starting at the south entrance near *Peace* and moving north, they are: SHERIDAN, GRANT, SHERMAN, SCOTT, FARRAGUT, NELSON, WILLIAM THE CONQUEROR, FREDERICK THE GREAT, EUGENE, MARLBOROUGH, WELLINGTON, WASHINGTON, CHARLES MARTEL, NAPOLEON, CAESAR, ALEXANDER, CYRUS, HANNIBAL, CHARLEMAGNE, and JACKSON.

The Northwest Pavilion
(Art and Science)

The paintings in the four lunettes and in the ceiling are by William de Leftwich Dodge. The subjects in the lunettes, clockwise from the west, are LITERATURE, MUSIC, SCIENCE, and ART. Ambition, considered the instigator of all human effort, is the subject of the ceiling painting.

Small circular reliefs representing the Four Seasons, executed by Bela Lyon Pratt, are in the four corners beneath the ceiling. The names of the seasons are listed below the paintings.

Wall plaques, clockwise from the northwest corner, bear the names: MUSIC, Venice, Berlin, Paris, SCIENCE, Babylon, Tyre, Carthage, ART, Thebes, Athens, Rhodes, LITERATURE, Greece, Italy, England.

The North Gallery (Learning)

The stained glass ceiling panels in the North Gallery contain the names of renowned painters, sculptors, musicians, scientists, theologians, physicians, and jurists. Designed in square panels, each section contains four inscribed tablets with the monogram LC in the center. "Learning" is inscribed in the central panel.

Beginning at the west end, the names are: HOLBEIN, VAN DYCK, RUBENS, MURILLO; REMBRANDT, THORWALDSEN, DURER, PALISSY; CORREGGIO, TITIAN, RAPHAEL, GUIDO RENI; PERUGINO, DA VINCI, APELLES, GIOTTO; PHIDIAS, LISZT, BACH, WAGNER; HAYDN, MENDELSSOHN, FARADAY, MOZART; AGASSIZ, DARWIN, COPERNICUS, HUMBOLDT; PLINY, EUCLID, CHANNING, PYTHAGORAS; EDWARDS, BOSSUET, ST. BERNARD, PASCAL; CHRYSOSTOM, ST. AUGUSTINE, HAHNEMANN, BOWDITCH; JENNER, HARVEY, AVICENNA, PARACELSUS; HIPPOCRATES, MARSHALL, MONTESQUIEU, STORY; BLACKSTONE, COKE, LYCURGUS, JUSTINIAN.

The Northeast Pavilion (Government)

The disc in the domed ceiling, designed by Elmer Ellsworth Garnsey, shows the Great Seal of the United States surrounded by allegorical emblems and objects that represent the North, South, East, and West sections of the country. Bordering the disc is a narrow blue band that is inscribed:

THAT THIS NATION, UNDER GOD, SHALL HAVE A NEW BIRTH OF FREEDOM; THAT GOVERNMENT OF THE PEOPLE, BY THE PEOPLE, FOR THE PEOPLE, SHALL NOT PERISH FROM THE EARTH

Abraham Lincoln, The Gettysburg Address, *Gettysburg, Pa., November 19, 1863*

The paintings in the lunettes, done by William Brantley Van Ingen, illustrate the seals of various executive departments of the United States Government. Each painting is devoted to two departments. A circular tablet divides the two parts, upon which are quotations from famous Americans.

West Lunette (State and Treasury Departments):

'TIS OUR TRUE POLICY TO STEER CLEAR OF PERMANENT ALLIANCE WITH ANY PORTION OF THE FOREIGN WORLD

George Washington, Farewell Address, *September 19, 1796*

LET OUR OBJECT BE OUR COUNTRY, OUR WHOLE COUNTRY, AND NOTHING BUT OUR COUNTRY

Daniel Webster, Address at Charlestown, Mass., June 17, 1825. *Cornerstone Ceremonies for Bunker Hill Monument.*

THANK GOD, I ALSO AM AN AMERICAN!

Daniel Webster, Address at Charlestown, Mass., June 17, 1843. *Dedication of Bunker Hill Monument.*

North Lunette (Justice and Post Office Departments):

EQUAL AND EXACT JUSTICE TO ALL MEN, OF WHATEVER STATE OR PERSUASION, RELIGIOUS OR POLITICAL: PEACE, COMMERCE, AND HONEST FRIENDSHIP WITH ALL NATIONS-ENTANGLING ALLIANCE WITH NONE

Thomas Jefferson, Inaugural Address, March 4, 1801

East Lunette (Agriculture and Interior Department):

THE AGRICULTURAL INTEREST OF THE COUNTRY IS CONNECTED WITH EVERY OTHER, AND SUPERIOR IN IMPORTANCE TO THEM ALL

Andrew Jackson, Message to Congress, December 8, 1829

U.S. Grant, Letter accepting nomination to the Presidency, May 29, 1868.

South Lunette (War and Navy Department):
THE AGGREGATE HAPPINESS OF SOCIETY IS, OR OUGHT TO BE,
THE END OF ALL GOVERNMENT
George Washington, Political Maxims

TO BE PREPARED FOR WAR IS ONE OF THE MOST EFFECTIVE
MEANS OF PRESERVING PEACE
George Washington, Speech to Congress, January 8, 1790.

Small circular reliefs representing the Four Seasons, executed by Bela Lyon Pratt, are in the four corners beneath the ceiling. The names of the seasons are beneath the paintings.

The Northeast Gallery (Building)

The stained glass ceiling panels in the Northeast Gallery contain the names of famous engineers and architects. "Building" is inscribed in the central panel. Beginning at the north end, the names are: BARNARD, SCHWEDLER, EADS, ROEBLING; JERVIS, VAUBAN, SMEATON, LAVALLY; STEPHENSON, ARCHIMEDES, RICHARDSON, HUNT; WALTER, BULFINCH, MANSARD, WREN, JONES; LABROUSTE, LESCOT, DUC, MICHELANGELO, DELORME; BRUNELLESCHI, SANSOVINO, VIGNOLA, BRAMANTE; PALLADIO, VITRUVIUS; ICTINUS, ANTHEMIUS.

The history of printing, one of the Jefferson Building's principal themes, is elaborately represented on the beautiful bronze doors of the Rare Book and Special Collections Division on the Jefferson Building's second floor. Printing in Europe is depicted on the door on the left, and printing in the New World on the right.

The Rare Book and Special Collections Division Reading Room

The Bronze Doors:

Left-hand door
    Top panel: device of Johann Fust and Peter Schoeffer
    Middle panel: emblem of Geofroy Tory
    Bottom panel: printers' mark of William Morris
Right-hand door
    Top panel: names of Juan Cromberger and Juan Pablos
    Center panel: names of Stephen Daye, William Nuthead, William Bradford
    Bottom panel: Bruce Rogers' printing device

The Rosenwald Room

The Lessing J. Rosenwald Collection of illustrated books, housed in the Rare Book and Special Collections Division, is one of the Library's greatest treasures. This room is modeled after Mr. Rosenwald's private gallery, the Alverthorpe Gallery in Jenkintown, Pennsylvania. Here he housed his collection of rare manuscripts and illustrated books, bequeathed to the Library of Congress in 1943. The bust of Orpheus on the wall is a full-size cast iron model of the head of the Orpheus Fountain in Stockholm. The sculptor is Carl Milles.

The Hispanic Room

The Hispanic Room occupies the Southeast Gallery, which was originally dedicated to "Invention," and contained the names of twenty-nine famous inventors from around the world. The stained glass ceiling, with "Invention" inscribed in the central panel, and the names are no longer visible because of the 1938 conversion of the gallery into the Hispanic Room. Beginning at the north end, the names are: BELL, WESTINGHOUSE, BESSEMER, EDISON, HOWE, HOE, ERICSSON, McCORMICK, GOODYEAR, WHITNEY, WHEATSTONE, MORSE, VAIL, WOOD, FITCH, JACQUARD, FULTON, ARKWRIGHT, HARGREAVES, CORLISS, TREVITHICK, NEWCOMEN, COOPER, WATT, STEVENS, MONTGOLFIER, DAGUERRE, GUTENBERG, SCHWARTZ.

In 1938, with the support of Archer M. Huntington, the room was converted into a reading room. It was designed by Paul Philippe Cret, the same architect who built both the Folger Shakespeare Library (across the street) and the Federal Reserve Building. In the northern vestibule are murals painted in 1941 by the Brazilian artist Cândido Portinari; they depict "Discovery of the Land," "Entry into the Forest," "Teaching of the Indians," and "Mining of Gold." In the central hall on the east wall over the windows are the names of eminent Hispanic literary figures: CERVANTES, CUERVO, PALMA, GONÇALVES DIAS, MONTALVO, RODÓ, HEREDIA. On the west wall: GARCÍA ICAZBALCETA, SARMIENTO, HOSTOS, DARIO, BELLO, MEDINA, CAMOËS. On the south wall is a colorful mural on steel that depicts the coat of arms of Christopher Columbus. Above the shield are the words "Por Castilla y por León" (For Castille and for León); below it, "Nuevo mundo halló Colón (For Columbus found a new world.") Beneath the mural is a marble tablet containing the following inscription:

THE HISPANIC FOUNDATION IN THE LIBRARY OF CONGRESS THIS CENTER FOR THE PURSUIT OF STUDIES IN SPANISH, PORTUGUESE, AND LATIN AMERICAN CULTURE HAS BEEN ESTABLISHED WITH THE GENEROUS COOPERATION OF THE HISPANIC SOCIETY OF AMERICA IN EXTENSION OF ITS SERVICE TO LEARNING.

The paintings in the four lunettes are by Robert L. Dodge and represent, clockwise from the north, AIR, EARTH, WATER, and FIRE. The ceiling disc, by Elmer E. Garnsey, represents the Sun, which is surrounded by medallions and cartouches that depict the four elements.

Small circular reliefs representing the Four Seasons, executed by Bela Lyon Pratt, are in the four corners beneath the ceiling. Such reliefs are in each of the four second floor pavilions, but the Latin instead of the English titles are used exclusively in this pavilion: *Hiems* or Winter, *Auctumnus* or Autumn, *Aestas* or Summer, and *Ver* or Spring.

Wall tablets, clockwise from the northeast corner, bear the names: AIR, Hermes, Zeus, and Iris; EARTH, Demeter, Hera, and Dionysus; WATER, Proteus, Galatea, and Poseidon; and FIRE, Hestia, Hephaestus, and Prometheus.

The South Gallery (Liberty)

The stained glass ceiling panels in the South Gallery contain the names of the signers of the Declaration of Independence. "Liberty" is inscribed in the central panel. Beginning at the east end, the names are:

HANCOCK	CLYMER	GWINNETT
GERRY	TAYLOR	HALL
ADAMS	SMITH	BARTLETT
PAINE/ADAMS	RODNEY	WALTON
CHASE	READ	ELLERY
CARROLL	STOCKTON	WHIPPLE
MCKEAN	HOPKINS	THORNTON
STONE	CLARK	HOOPER
PACA	WITHERSPOON	HEWES
MORRIS	HART	WYTHE
FLOYD	HOPKINSON	LEE
LEWIS	MIDDLETON	PENN
LIVINGSTON	RUTLEDGE	BRAXTON
MORTON	LYNCH	JEFFERSON
MORRIS	HEYWARD	NELSON
FRANKLIN	WOLCOTT	LEE
RUSH	SHERMAN	HARRISON
ROSS	WILLIAMS	
WILSON	HUNTINGTON	

THOTH

BRAHMA

TS'ANG CHIEH

CADMUS

NABU

ITZAMNA

The John Adams Building

❊ ❊

The history of the written word is depicted in the bronze doors of the Adams Building, the work of sculptor Lee Lawrie. These figures on the center doors at the east (Third Street) entrance are repeated on the two flanking doors at the west (Second Street) entrance.

Pages 74–75: The John Adams Building opened its doors to the public in 1939. Its dignified, classical exterior is faced with white Georgia marble.

In 1928, at the urging of Librarian of Congress Herbert Putnam, Congress authorized the purchase of land directly east of the Library's Main Building for the construction of an Annex Building. The bill was sponsored by Robert Luce, chairman of the House Committee on the Library. On June 13, 1930, $6,500,00 was appropriated for the building's construction, for a tunnel connecting it to the Main Building, and for changes in the east front of the Main Building, including the construction of a Rare Book Room. An additional appropriation approved on June 6, 1935, brought the total authorization to $8,226,457.

The simple classical structure was intended as a functional and efficient bookstack "encircled with work spaces." David Lynn, the Architect of the Capitol, commissioned the Washington architectural firm of Pierson & Wilson to design the building, with Alexander Buel Trowbridge as consulting architect. The contract stipulated completion by June 24, 1938, but the building was not ready for occupancy until December 2, 1938. The move of the Card Division started on December 12, and it opened its doors to the public in the new building on January 3, 1939. The building is five stories in height above ground, with the fifth story set back 35 feet. It contains 180 miles of shelving (compared to 104 miles in the Jefferson Building) and can hold ten million volumes. There are 12 tiers of stacks, extending from the cellar to the fourth floor. Each tier provides about 13 acres of shelf space.

On April 13, 1976, in a ceremony at the Jefferson Memorial marking the birthday of Thomas Jefferson, President Ford signed into law the act to change the name of the Library of Congress Annex Building to the Library of Congress Thomas Jefferson Building. On June 13, 1980, the structure acquired its present name, which honors John Adams, the man of letters and president of the United States who in 1800 approved the law establishing the Library of Congress.

The dignified exterior of the Adams Building is faced with white Georgia marble. Today, the building's decorative style is widely admired for elements inspired by the Exposition des Arts Decoratifs held in Paris in 1925 and the use of new materials such as acoustical block, formica, vitrolit, and glass tubing. Decorative features and metalwork in the first floor lobbies and corridors and in the fifth floor lobbies and reading rooms are worth special note.

THE WEST AND EAST ENTRANCE DOORS

The history of the written word is depicted in sculpted figures by Lee Lawrie on the bronze doors at the west (Second Street) and east (Third Street) entrances. The center doors at the west entrance contain six figures, which are repeated on the flanking doors of the east entrance. The figures are:

HERMES, the messenger of the gods
ODIN, the Viking-Germanic god of war and creator of the runic alphabet
OGMA, the Irish god who invented the Gaelic alphabet
ITZAMA, god of the Mayans
QUETZALCOATL, the god of the Aztecs
SEQUOYAH, an American Indian

The two flanking doors of the west entrance depict six other figures who are part of the history of the written word. The figures, repeated on the center door of the east entrance, are:

THOTH, an Egyptian god
TS'ANG CHIEH, the Chinese patron of writing
NABU, an Akkadian god
BRAHMA, the Indian god
CADMUS, the Greek sower of dragon's teeth
TAHMURATH, a hero of the ancient Persians

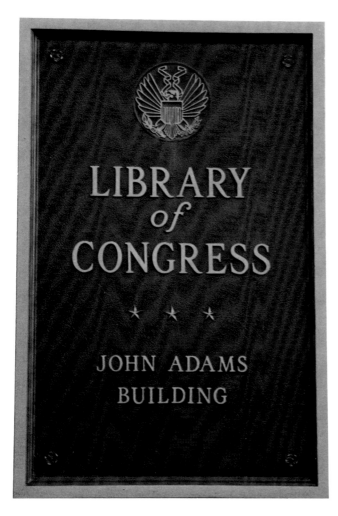

Plaque on Second Street, S.E. in front of the Adams Building. Today's Adams Building was called the Annex Building until 1976 and the Jefferson Building from 1976 to 1980.

THE INDEPENDENCE AVENUE (SOUTH) DOORS

A sculpted stairway, complete with stylized owls and elaborate lamps, leads to the southern entrance on Independence Avenue. This entrance, though not presently used, was originally designed for the United States Copyright Office. Two figures are depicted on the doors. The male figure on the left door, beneath the seal of the United States, represents physical labor. The female figure on the right door, beneath the open book, represents intellectual labor.

THE NORTH READING ROOM (CHAUCER MURALS)

The murals by Ezra Winter in the North Reading Room illustrate the characters of Geoffrey Chaucer's Canterbury Tales. The procession of characters on the west and east walls presents the Pilgrims in very nearly the order Chaucer introduced them in the Prologue to the *Canterbury Tales.* The exception is Chaucer himself, whom the artist has interjected in the midst of the procession on the west wall. The Pilgrims, from left to right, on the west wall, are:

THE MILLER, IN THE LEAD, PIPING THE BAND OUT OF SOUTHWARK; THE HOST OF TABARD INN; THE KNIGHT, FOLLOWED BY HIS SON, THE YOUNG SQUIRE, ON A WHITE PALFREY; A YEOMAN; THE DOCTOR OF PHYSIC; CHAUCER, RIDING WITH HIS BACK TO THE OBSERVER, AS HE TALKS TO THE LAWYER; THE CLERK OF OXENFORD, READING HIS BELOVED CLASSICS; THE MANCIPLE; THE SAILOR; THE PRIORESS; THE NUN; AND THREE PRIESTS.

The procession continues on the east wall with:

THE MERCHANT, WITH HIS FLEMISH BEAVER HAT AND FORKED BEARD; THE
FRIAR; THE MONK; THE FRANKLIN; THE WIFE OF BATH; THE PARSON AND HIS
BROTHER THE PLOUGHMAN, RIDING SIDE BY SIDE; THE WEAVER; THE DYER; THE
ARRAS-MAKER; THE CARPENTER; THE HABERDASHER; THE COOK; THE SUM-
MONER; THE PARDONER; AND, AT THE END OF THE PROCESSION, THE REEVE.

The small rectangular painting above the clock on the north wall has
the Prologue of the *Tales* as its subject, with the following quotation from
the beginning:

WHAN THAT APRILLE WITH HIS SHOURES SOOTE
THE DROGHTE OF MARCH HATH PERCED TO THE ROOTE,
AND BATHED EVERY VEYNE IN SWICH LICOUR
OF WHICH VERTU ENGENDRED IS THE FLOUR;
WHAN ZEPHIRUS EEK WITH HIS SWETE BREETH
INSPIRED HATH IN EVERY HOLT AND HEETH
THE TENDRE CROPPES, AND THE YONGE SONNE
HATH IN THE RAM HIS HALVE COURS YRONNE,
AND SMALE FOWELES MAKEN MELODYE
THAT SLEPEN AL THE NYGHT WITH OPEN YE
(SO PRIKETH HEM NATURE IN HIR CORAGES);
THANNE LONGEN FOLK TO GOON ON PILGRIMAGES ...

A lunette with three musicians, on the south wall under the reference desk,
inspired by the Prologue of the *Franklin's Tale,* is signed and dated, like the
painting on the north wall, and is based on the following quotation from the
introductory verse to the Prologue:

THISE OLDE GENTIL BRITOUNS IN HIR DAYES
OF DIVERSE AVENTURES MADEN LAYES,
RYMEYED IN HIR FIRSTE BRITON TONGE;
WHICHE LAYES WITH HIR INSTRUMENTZ THEY SONGE,
OR ELLES REDDEN HEM, OR HIR PLESAUNCE ...

Murals by Ezra Winter also decorate the South Reading Room. The theme for these four murals is drawn from Thomas Jefferson's writings, which are inscribed on the paintings and reflect Jefferson's thoughts on Freedom, Labor, the Living Generation, Education, and Democratic Government. The characters and costumes depicted are those of Jefferson's time. A portrait of Jefferson with his residence, Monticello, in the background is in the lunette above the reference desk at the north end of the room; the words in the lower right-hand corner explain that THIS ROOM IS DEDICATED TO THOMAS JEFFERSON.

On the left half of the panel on the east wall, Jefferson's view of Freedom is depicted:

THE GROUND OF LIBERTY IS TO BE GAINED BY INCHES. WE MUST BE CONTENTED TO SECURE WHAT WE CAN GET FROM TIME TO TIME AND ETERNALLY PRESS FORWARD FOR WHAT IS YET TO GET. IT TAKES TIME TO PERSUADE MEN TO DO EVEN WHAT IS FOR THEIR OWN GOOD.

Jefferson to Rev. Charles Clay, January 27, 1790

Jefferson's views on Labor, also on the east wall, are taken from his *Notes on Virginia:*

THOSE WHO LABOR IN THE EARTH ARE THE CHOSEN PEOPLE OF GOD, IF HE EVER HAD A CHOSEN PEOPLE, WHOSE BREASTS HE HAS MADE THE PECULIAR DEPOSITS FOR SUBSTANTIAL AND GENUINE VIRTUE. IT IS THE FOCUS IN WHICH HE KEEPS ALIVE THAT SACRED FIRE WHICH OTHERWISE MIGHT NOT ESCAPE FROM THE EARTH.

From Notes on Virginia, *1782*

On the south wall, the panel over the clock contains a quotation about the Living Generation:

THE EARTH BELONGS ALWAYS TO THE LIVING GENERATION. THEY MAY MANAGE IT THEN AND WHAT PROCEEDS FROM IT AS THEY PLEASE DURING THEIR USUFRUCT. THEY ARE MASTERS TOO OF THEIR OWN PERSONS AND CONSEQUENTLY MAY GOVERN THEM AS THEY PLEASE.

Jefferson to James Madison, September 6, 1789

On the left half of the panel on the west wall, Jefferson's view of Education is illustrated:

EDUCATE AND INFORM THE MASS OF THE PEOPLE. ENABLE THEM TO SEE THAT IT IS THEIR INTEREST TO PRESERVE PEACE AND ORDER, AND THEY WILL PRESERVE THEM. ENLIGHTEN THE PEOPLE GENERALLY, AND TYRANNY AND OPPRESSION OF THE BODY AND MIND WILL VANISH LIKE EVIL SPIRITS AT THE DAWN OF DAY.

Jefferson to James Madison, December 20, 1787 (first two sentences); Jefferson to P. S. Dupont de Nemours, April 24, 1816 (last sentence).

Thomas Jefferson's view of Education is illustrated in this mural by Ezra Winter in the South Reading Room on the top floor of the Adams Building. Other murals dedicated to Jefferson decorate all of the reading room's walls.

E PEOPLE ~ ENABLE THEM TO SEE THAT IT IS THEIR INTEREST TO
WILL PRESERVE THEM · ENLIGHTEN THE PEOPLE GENERALLY AND
Y AND MIND WILL VANISH LIKE EVIL SPIRITS AT THE DAWN OF DAY.

Jefferson's views on Democratic Government, also on the west wall, are illustrated:

THE PEOPLE OF EVERY COUNTRY ARE THE ONLY SAFE GUARDIANS OF THEIR OWN RIGHTS, AND ARE THE ONLY INSTRUMENTS WHICH CAN BE USED FOR THEIR DESTRUCTION. IT IS AN AXIOM IN MY MIND THAT OUR LIBERTY CAN NEVER BE SAFE BUT IN THE HANDS OF THE PEOPLE THEMSELVES, THAT, TOO, OF THE PEOPLE WITH A CERTAIN DEGREE OF INSTRUCTION.

Jefferson to John Wyche, May 19, 1809 (first sentence);
Jefferson to George Washington, January 4, 1786 (second sentence).

KNOWLEDGE WILL FOREVER
GOVERN IGNORANCE:
AND A PEOPLE WHO MEAN
TO BE THEIR OWN GOVERNOURS,
MUST ARM THEMSELVES
WITH THE POWER
WHICH KNOWLEDGE GIVES.

James Madison

The James Madison Memorial Building

❀ ❀

This quotation from James Madison about the importance of knowledge is on the exterior wall on the left side of the James Madison Memorial Building entrance.

Pages 84–85: Opened in 1980, the Madison Building is this nation's official memorial to James Madison.

In 1957, Librarian of Congress L. Quincy Mumford initiated studies for a third Library building. Congress appropriated planning funds for that structure, today's James Madison Memorial Building, in 1960, and construction was approved by an act of Congress on October 19, 1965 that authorized an appropriation of $75 million. Excavation and foundation work began in June 1971, and work on the superstructure was completed in 1976. The cornerstone, inscribed with the date 1974, was laid on March 8, 1974. Dedication ceremonies were held on April 24, 1980, and the building actually opened on May 28, 1980.

The Madison Building serves both as the Library's third major structure and as this nation's official memorial to James Madison, the "father" of the U.S. Constitution and the Bill of Rights and the fourth president of the United States.

That a major Library of Congress building should also become a memorial to James Madison is fitting, for the institution's debt to him is considerable. In 1783, as a member of the Continental Congress, Madison became the first sponsor of the idea of a library for Congress by proposing a list of books that would be useful to legislators, an effort that preceded by seventeen years the establishment of the Library of Congress. In 1815, Madison was president of the United States and a keen observer when the library of his close personal friend and collaborator, Thomas Jefferson, became the foundation of a renewed Library of Congress. Like Jefferson, he was a man of books and an enlightened statesman who believed the power of knowledge was essential for individual liberty and democratic government.

The Architect of the Capitol was charged with the responsibility for the construction of the the Madison Building under the direction of the Senate and House Building Commissions and the Joint Committee on the Library and in consultation with a committee appointed by the American Institute of Architects. Plans for the Madison Memorial Hall were developed in consultation with the James Madison Memorial Commission. The total authorization for construction eventually was increased to $130,675,000.

Modern in style, the Madison Building was designed by the firm of De-Witt, Poor, and Shelton, Associated Architects. When it opened, it was one of the three largest public buildings in the Washington, D.C. area (the others were the Pentagon and the F.B.I. Building). It contains 2,100,000 square feet with 1,500,000 square feet of assignable space.

Over the main entrance is a four-story relief in bronze, "Falling Books," by Frank Eliscu. Off the entrance hall to the immediate left is the James Madison Memorial Hall, which has eight quotations from Madison on its walls (see below). A heroic statue by Walker K. Hancock in the center portrays Madison as a young man in his thirties, holding in his right hand volume 83 of the *Encyclopédie Méthodique,* which was published in Paris between 1782 and 1832. At the end of the entrance hall, above the doorways to the Manuscript Reading Room and the Manuscript Division office, are a pair of bronze medallions by Robert Alexander Weinman. The one on the left shows the profile of Madison and the one on the right depicts Madison at work.

Ten quotations from the writings of James Madison adorn the outside walls of the Madison Building. Two are located on each side of the main entrance on Independence Avenue. On the left side of the main entrance:

KNOWLEDGE WILL FOREVER GOVERN IGNORANCE: AND A PEOPLE WHO MEAN TO BE THEIR OWN GOVERNOURS, MUST ARM THEMSELVES WITH THE POWER WHICH KNOWLEDGE GIVES.

Madison to W. T. Barry, August 4, 1822

On the right side of the entrance:

WHAT SPECTACLE CAN BE MORE EDIFYING OR MORE SEASONABLE, THAN THAT OF LIBERTY & LEARNING, EACH LEANING ON THE OTHER FOR THEIR MUTUAL & SUREST SUPPORT?

Madison to W. T. Barry, August 4, 1822

JAMES MADISON MEMORIAL HALL

The names of the individuals responsible for the planning, legislation, design, and construction of the Madison Building (1960–1980) are inscribed on the wall to the left just inside the building's front doors. Included are members of the Joint Committee on the Library, the Senate Office Building Committee, the House Office Building Committee, the chairman of the James Madison Memorial Commission, Librarians of Congress, Architects of the Capitol, Associate Architects, and Builders.

Eight quotations from James Madison were incised in the teakwood panels of the Memorial Hall by Constantine L. Seferlis. Beginning on the wall on the left just inside the entrance and proceeding to the right around Madison Memorial Hall, the quotations are:

LEARNED INSTITUTIONS OUGHT TO BE FAVORITE OBJECTS WITH EVERY FREE PEOPLE. THEY THROW THAT LIGHT OVER THE PUBLIC MIND WHICH IS THE BEST SECURITY AGAINST CRAFTY & DANGEROUS ENCROACHMENTS ON THE PUBLIC LIBERTY

Madison to W. T. Barry, August 4, 1822

WHAT SPECTACLE
CAN BE MORE EDIFYING
OR MORE SEASONABLE,
THAN THAT OF
LIBERTY & LEARNING,
EACH LEANING ON THE OTHER
FOR THEIR MUTUAL
& SUREST SUPPORT ?

James Madison

Like his friend Thomas Jefferson, James Madison was a man of books who believed that the power of knowledge was essential for individual liberty and democratic government. In 1783, as a member of the Continental Congress, Madison proposed a legislative library and drew up a list of more than 300 desirable books. His eloquent "liberty & learning" statement, inscribed on the right side of the Madison Building entrance, is from an August 22, 1822 letter to W. T. Barry.

THE HAPPY UNION OF THESE STATES IS A WONDER: THEIR CONSTITUTION A MIRACLE: THEIR EXAMPLE THE HOPE OF LIBERTY THOUGHOUT THE WORLD

"Outline Notes," September 1829

THE ESSENCE OF GOVERNMENT IS POWER; AND POWER, LODGED AS IT MUST BE IN HUMAN HANDS, WILL EVER BE LIABLE TO ABUSE

Speech before the Virginia State Constitutional Convention, December 1 1829

EQUAL LAWS PROTECTING EQUAL RIGHTS ARE THE BEST GUARANTEE OF LOYALTY & LOVE OF COUNTRY

Madison to Jacob de la Motta, August, 1820

AS A MAN IS SAID TO HAVE A RIGHT TO HIS PROPERTY, HE MAY BE EQUALLY SAID TO HAVE A PROPERTY IN HIS RIGHTS

National Gazette, *March 29, 1792*

WAR CONTAINS MUCH FOLLY, AS WELL AS WICKEDNESS, THAT MUCH IS TO BE HOPED FROM THE PROGRESS OF REASON; AND IF ANYTHING IS TO BE HOPED, EVERY THING OUGHT TO BE TRIED

National Gazette, *February 2, 1792*

THE FREE SYSTEM OF GOVERNMENT WE HAVE ESTABLISHED IS SO CONGENIAL WITH REASON, WITH COMMON SENSE, AND WITH A UNIVERSAL FEELING THAT IT MUST PRODUCE APPROBATION AND A DESIRE OF IMITATION, AS AVENUES MAY BE FOUND FOR TRUTH TO THE KNOWLEDGE OF NATIONS

Madison to Pierre E. Duponceau, January 23, 1826

THE SAFETY AND HAPPINESS OF SOCIETY ARE THE OBJECTS AT WHICH ALL POLITICAL INSTITUTIONS AIM, AND TO WHICH ALL SUCH INSTITUTIONS MUST BE SACRIFICED

Federalist, No. 43, January 1788

Author's Note

This book is intended primarily for visitors to the Jefferson, Adams, and Madison Buildings. The wording of inscriptions and quotations and the spelling of proper names corresponds to what the visitor will see "on these walls" and occasionally differs slightly from what one finds in the cited sources. In most cases, when a source is cited it is to a general reference which interested readers can pursue further, using the Index and Guide to Names as a starting point. The Biblical references are to the Authorized King James Version of the Holy Bible.

Each of the Library of Congress's buildings—but particularly the Jefferson Building—is a wonderful "do-it-yourself" educational experience which this book is meant to enhance. I also hope it inspires historians to undertake much-needed work on the Jefferson Building's art, architecture, and iconography.

Acknowledgements

I am heavily indebted to Herbert Small's invaluable *Handbook of the New Library of Congress in Washington* (Boston, 1897), a contemporary guidebook that Small prepared after consultation with many of the people responsible for the construction and decoration of the Jefferson Building. Valuable information was found in records in the Library of Congress Archives in the Manuscript Division, Library of Congress, where John Knowlton, specialist in Library of Congress history and archives, provided expert guidance.

Many other Library of Congress staff members have helped with this project, which I have worked on intermittently for more than ten years. Anne Boni, Sharon Green, Pat White, and Michael Thompson assisted with the preparation of the manuscript; Alan Bisbort provided research assistance and editorial help; and Maurvene D. Williams prepared the index and guide to names.

In the summer of 1988, intern Barbara S. C. Clark helped with research and fact-checking. Barbara Wolanin, Office of the Architect of the Capitol, and Ford Peatross of the Library's Prints and Photographs Division reviewed the completed manuscript and offered encouragement and useful suggestions. My thanks to all.

Further Reading

Cole, John Y. *For Congress and the Nation: A Chronological History of the Library of Congress.* Washington: Library of Congress, 1979.

Cole, John Y. *Jefferson's Legacy: A Brief History of the Library of Congress.* Washington: Library of Congress, 1993.

Cole, John Y. "A National Monument for a National Library: Ainsworth Rand Spofford and the New Library of Congress, 1871–1897, *Records of the Columbia Historical Society of Washington, D.C., 1971–1972.* Ed. by Francis Coleman Rosenberger. Washington: Columbia Historical Society, 1973.

Cole, John Y. "Smithmeyer & Pelz: Embattled Architects of the Library of Congress," *Quarterly Journal of the Library of Congress* 29: (October 1972): 282–307.

Hilker, Helen-Anne. *Ten First Street Southeast: Congress Builds a Library, 1886–1897.* Washington: Library of Congress, 1980.

"Madison Building Dedication Set for April 24." *Library of Congress Information Bulletin* 39 (April 18, 1980): 129–133.

Nelson, Josephus and Judith Farley. *Full Circle: Ninety Years of Service in the Main Reading Room.* Washington: Library of Congress, 1991.

Reynolds, Charles B. *The Library of Congress and the Interior Decorations.* Washington: Foster & Reynolds, 1897.

Roberts, Martin. "The Annex of the Library of Congress." *Report of the Librarian of Congress for the Fiscal Year Ending June 30, 1937.* Washington: Government Printing Office, 1937, pp. 354–357.

Scott, Pamela and Antoinette J. Lee. *Buildings of the District of Columbia.* New York: Oxford University Press, 1993.

Small, Herbert, comp. *Handbook of the New Library of Congress in Washington.* Boston: Curtis & Cameron, 1897. Includes essays on "Architecture, Sculpture and Painting" by Charles Caffin, and on "The Function of a National Library" by Ainsworth Rand Spofford. A revised edition, published under the title *The Library of Congress: Its Architecture and Decoration,* edited by Henry Hope Reed, was published by W. W. Norton in 1982.

Walter, Emily L'Oiseau. *A Complete Collection of the Quotations and Inscriptions in the Library of Congress.* Eleventh Revised Edition. Baltimore, 1930.

Index and Guide to Names

ISBN 0-16-045301-1